Discerning Your Spiritual Gifts

DISCERNING YOUR SPIRITUAL GIFTS

LLOYD EDWARDS

COWLEY PUBLICATIONS
Cambridge ✦ Boston
Massachusetts

Published in the United States of America by Cowley
Publications, a division of the Society of St. John the Evangelist.
No portion of this book may be reproduced, stored in or
introduced into a retrieval system, or transmitted, in any form or
by any means—including photocopying—without the prior
written permission of Cowley Publications, except in the case of
brief quotations embodied in critical articles and reviews.

Library of Congress Cataloging in Publication Data:
Edwards, Lloyd, 1941–
    Discerning your spiritual gifts / Lloyd Edwards.
        p.   cm.
    Bibliography: p.
    ISBN: 0-936384-65-4
    1. Gifts, Spiritual. I. Title.
BT767.3.E38 1988
234'.13–dc 19   88-25728

Editor: Cynthia Shattuck
Cover Design: Vicki Black
Cover art is a detail of Melon Tapestry by Kaffe Fassett.

This book is printed on acid-free paper and was produced in the
United States of America.

Seventh printing

Cowley Publications
28 Temple Place   •   Boston, Massachusetts 02111
1-800-225-1534   •   http://www.cowley.org

In memory of
Terry Holmes

CONTENTS

PREFACE

Recently I was asked to present a spiritual autobiography, a recollection of my life and how my life experiences shaped my theological growth. As I prepared it, I was surprised to see a common theme running through my whole life. It began when I was very young and my mother read Holy Scripture to me each evening. Her favorite passage was the twelfth chapter of the Epistle to the Romans, one of the most important places in the New Testament dealing with spiritual gifts. The theme developed through my puzzlement and confusion about my own gifts, my dilettante-way of trying to use them all and more, of trying to use gifts that I wanted but did not have, of taking for granted and not using gifts that I did have. It developed even further through the teaching and ministry of the Rev. Robert K. Pierce, who taught me most of what I know about spiritual gifts, and who confronted me to be assertive in discovering, claiming, and using my own. And it continued to develop, though it has not ended, with the people of Trinity Cathedral, with whom I delight in sharing the ministry to which we are called. They use their considerable gifts in marvelous ways and claim their own unique ministries with grace and conviction. I thank God for these people, for their struggles and their willingness to share them, and most of all for their humor and passion for Christ.

I have written this book to meet three needs in a reader. The first is a need for clear thinking and a coherent point of view about spiritual gifts. I do not claim that mine is the only reasonable or the only biblical point of view on this subject; my claim is simply that I have worked with and thought about the subject for some years and have developed a way of thinking about the subject which is coherent and which has been helpful to many.

The second need is to find one's own gifts. The ways presented here for finding one's own gifts assume that we can know what our gifts are in much the same way we know other things about ourselves: by observing and hearing the observations of others, thinking, analyzing and synthesizing, coming to a conjecture, and then testing and trying out what we have conjectured. I have also assumed that, while the list of gifts found in Scripture is important, different gifts are necessary for the different circumstances of our day. Thus we need ways of discerning gifts which go beyond those gifts listed in Scripture.

The third need is to help others find their gifts. Those who work as spiritual guides know that there are many ways to find one's gifts. What I present here is not new, but it may be helpful to have an explicit process laid out carefully, and to have tried and tested designs for classes and workshops. I encourage those who work as spiritual guides to consider the workshop format for the task of discerning gifts. There is great value in the interplay of viewpoints and abilities among adult learners, and I have found the workshops to be much more exciting and stimulating, and more productive of real discernment about gifts, than the same processes done one-on-one.

In writing this book, I have found no solution to the current language-gender problem. I have chosen to use both genders in rough alternation, believing that such usage may bring small but salutary shocks to the reader and the writer which will challenge any remaining gender-biased thinking due to language.

J. Lloyd Edwards
Trinity Cathedral

ASKING THE RIGHT QUESTIONS

Mary is a woman in her late thirties. She is well trained as a speech and hearing therapist and has a good job. She is married, and she and her husband have two children. She enjoys her work and her family but feels that they are not enough to make her life whole. Something is missing. Mary is looking for something deeper, more challenging in life.

Harrison is retiring from a rewarding career as a corporate executive. He is wondering what his alternatives are, and is concerned about the "retire, vegetate, and die" pattern that he has observed many of his colleagues follow.

Al is a research geologist. He is successful in his career and has a fine family but recently has noticed a certain emptiness in his life. He is a devout churchman, attends and pledges, participates in most of the programs that the church offers. He feels that his emptiness is somehow spiritual, but is not sure of that. As he puts it, "I'm doing everything the church offers. If my problem were a spiritual one, I'm sure it would have been mentioned in church some time or other."

Bill is a high school senior. He looks at the many possible career opportunities and wonders where he fits in. His father wants him to follow in his steps as a lawyer and corporate executive. His mother wants him to be a doctor as her father was. Bill thinks that neither is right for him, but doesn't have any specific alternative to present to them.

Joan recently emerged from a struggle with depression. After her husband died, she struggled alone for a while, then sought help from a psychotherapist. And after some months of therapy she has made changes in her life which have eased the feelings of depression that were troubling her. She feels that she is ready to terminate therapy but feels that there should be something else to life, something that transcends therapy. She is ready for broader personal growth and is not sure where to look for it.

Sam is in his mid-thirties. He is gifted in many areas, and is interested in them all—music, art, mathematics, writing. He has tried a number of vocations, but seems unable to concentrate on one for fear of neglecting the others. He is dissatisfied with what he has accomplished, but still does not choose one direction for his creative life. He describes himself jokingly as a dilettante and wonders aloud what he is going to be when he grows up.

Heather is the adult child of alcoholic parents. Through a group she has discovered the source of much of the pain she has experienced in her life, and through therapy she has worked through many of the self-defeating patterns of behavior she had learned. Now she wonders, "Is that all there is—just overcoming negative training, just muck? Isn't there anything positive that I got from the experience of growing up in an alcoholic family—any strengths, any gifts? Where is God's grace in my experience?"

These people—Mary, Harrison, Al, Bill, Joan, Sam, and Heather—and many others may not have heard of spiritual gifts. Although spiritual gifts have a prominent place in the New Testament, they have typically been neglected in Christian teaching, or if they were taught, may have been taught in such a way that they seemed inaccessible or irrelevant to the average Christian.

Yet all seven could benefit from a knowledge of their gifts. Mary might find something that would challenge her to new growth in ways that her work does not touch. Harrison might find abilities and interests in his life which give him new energy and personal fulfillment, and which he now has the opportunity to pursue. Al might find that his emptiness is spiritual in nature and that there is a remedy for it within the Christian tradition. Bill might discover something new about himself which will help him to make decisions about his college major, decisions that he can present to his parents. Joan may find a way of growth which builds on what she learned in therapy, yet which concentrates on her strengths rather than on her problems. Sam may find that there is one great calling for him that either combines many of his talents or which is so fulfilling that he can gladly give up others to pursue it. And Heather may find the one great gift that grew like a flower in the barnyard of her childhood experience and may yet pluck the flower for herself.

After many years of working with people in counseling, learning about and using my own spiritual gifts, and helping others learn and use their gifts, I am convinced that there is a major gap in Christian teaching. We have helped people to learn the lore of the faith. We have helped them practice moral living. We have helped them solve their problems of living, to pray, to nurture loving relationships. And yet we have *not* helped them find precisely what it is that God made them for, what it is that will give them the most profound joy imaginable.

In this chapter I would like to tell of the importance of spiritual gifts by describing the dimensions of the gap that they fill. By asking the right questions, questions to which the answer is "spiritual gifts", we may understand their real importance.

The first question is: What does God want of me?

One of the pleasures of my job is talking with people who are on a spiritual journey, journeying toward God through Christ. Often they ask, "What is my next step?" They have been Christians for many years. They have read Scripture, prayed, lived moral lives. And now they are ready to move deeper into the journey.

Typically they have moved through three decision points in their journey, decision points that are common to most Christians.[1] The first decision is the fundamental decision for God. It is what Tillich might have described as "accepting God's acceptance of me." It is what Dag Hammarskjold meant when he wrote in his spiritual journal *Markings* of saying "YES" to God. Growth in Christ is lifelong; much of it is slow, often tedious. It does not often issue in dramatic breakthroughs or heroic reversals. But I believe that there is a time, perhaps many times, in one's life when we must make the basic choice for God—not "Do I believe in God?" as a matter of intellectual assent, but "Am I God's person?" It is a question of fidelity and obedience, a matter of accepting a relationship with God at the deepest level of which we are capable. We may be faced with the decision many times, but all of us face it at least once.

The second decision is about the basic vocational covenants of life: baptism, marriage, parenting, work, celibacy, ordination or lay ministry. These are pledges of fidelity to a role or lifestyle, pledges which have the weight of divinity to them. It is not so much that "God wants me to marry this person", but that, once I have made those vows, they are to be taken seriously and affect my relationship with God. They are of a profoundly serious character, and we usually signify this by making them in the name of God.

The third kind of decision has to do with the circumstances into which we are thrown. I mean that we are called to do justice and kindness, to be loving and creative, in the day-to-day situations in which we find ourselves. If I see a man fall down in the street, I have a calling to help him. This call would be incumbent on anyone who was in the same situation as I.

Yet these first three answers to the question, "What does God want of me?" all have in them elements of anonymity Everyone is called to the fundamental covenant, and the answer "yes" or "no" leaves little room for the question of our personal uniqueness. All who are baptized and all who are married make similar vows, depending on the tradition in which they wed. All who are in a particular situation have a similar calling.

When we ask the question, "What does God want of *me*—not of one who is married, or of one who is baptized, but of *me*, created unique in all the world?", then we get to the fourth answer to the question. God wants me to use the gifts bestowed upon me to do God's will. My gifts are unique. They are a product of my genetic inheritance, of my experience, of my particular likes and dislikes, of my particular wounds and sufferings. No one else has exactly the same combination of these as I. And it is precisely this combination—all of it—that I am called to use in God's service. When we have discovered our gifts, we have discovered what is unique about our call from God; we have discovered that which most personally relates us to our creator.

Furthermore, the shape of my responses to the first three calls of God is greatly influenced by my particular gifts. My "yes" to God is partly an offering of my gifts for God's use, and the particular gifts I have will influence the particular way in which I respond to God's call. My gifts shape the nature of my marriage or celibacy, of my lay or priestly calling, of the way that I raise my children or do my work.

My assumption in these pages is that God has created the world, and that the willfulness of humans has led to the fall. I assume that God is acting to redeem the whole world, and that God has done this and is doing this now by calling together a people, a community of faith and action—first the Israelites, later the Christians. God's purpose is to re-unite and reconcile the world, and whoever works toward that cause is God's person. Thus we are confronted with the activity of God in the world, and our choice is to be part of the work of redemption or not. If we choose to do so, we have the gifts already; if not, we simply get what we have chosen. We will not be a part of the work that God is doing at the heart of the world; we choose boredom, spiritual ennui, alienation, loneliness, finally death.

The catechism of the Episcopal Church's prayer book begins with these questions and answers, which touch on a further dimension of the discernment of our spiritual gifts.

Q. *What are we by nature?*

A. *We are part of God's creation, made in the image of God.*

Q. *What does it mean to be made in the image of God?*

A. *It means that we are free to make choices: to love, to create, to reason, and to live in harmony with creation and with God.*

The emphasis on creativity and reason in the context of love, and on the freedom to make choices, provides a solid context for the discernment and use of gifts. We can use our reason to discover them and our creativity in finding an outlet for them. Discernment is not an esoteric or private action, but one open to our reasonable judgment. Similarly, we can choose whether and how to use them. The process of learning and using gifts is largely a process of choosing among options and becoming aware of a wider range of options than before. The process of learning and using gifts is not different from the process of salvation itself; in our choosing lies our wholeness.

This takes us to the second question: Where is my deepest joy?

My deepest joy comes in using the gifts God has given me to do the divine work in the world. When I do this, I have a sense of "doing what I was created to do, being who I was created to be." I will write later about the relationship between wounds, healing and spiritual gifts; for now, it is sufficient to say that our wounds and gifts are related in such a way that when we use our gifts, our own wounds are healed a bit more than before. Thus there is great fulfillment and healing in the use of our gifts. They can lead us into deep joy.

In the traditions of Western Christianity, sin has always played a central role. The spiritual journey has been seen as a struggle against sin, a "spiritual warfare" against the powers of evil. While there is a great deal of truth in this metaphor, it has led many people to believe that the struggle with sin is the whole spiritual struggle, or at least that they must have won the final battle with sin before they can begin to do the work to which they have been called. The oft-heard comment, "I have to get my life straightened out before I could possibly be of help to anyone else," reflects this scrupulosity and reveals a view of sinfulness that is profoundly unbiblical. This sense of unworthiness is not the Good News of the Gospel; it is bad news. The fact that one has been given spiritual gifts can be the form that the Good News takes for a person who feels unworthy. It can become the source for deep joy and the impetus to do God's work. The fact of spiritual gifts undercuts the negative self-image of many people; if I am gifted, am I not already worthy? Has God not entrusted me with something precious and valuable? Doesn't God love me, not merely in a general and anonymous way, but in a specific and concrete way, a way unique to me?

The second reason that we find joy in using our spiritual gifts is the simple direct experience of pleasure we have when we do something well and feel fulfilled in doing it. When we use our gifts we are doing what we were created to do, being who we are created to be. We are likely to be more confident, more centered, we are more likely to know instinctively what our next move is, than when we are trying to do something which does not call out our gifts. Someone watching us use our gifts may have a sense of the uncanny, as some do in listening to a great musician perform her favorite work. The gifted person, on the other hand, often takes the gift for granted, sometimes assuming that "anyone could do the same thing—you just have to put your mind to it." Often people say, after discovering their gifts, "I have been doing that for years; I knew that I did it well, and I knew that I received great satisfaction in doing it; but I never thought of it as a gift from God." They may be disappointed to discover that they had been using their gifts all along, for they had perhaps hoped to find something new and exotic buried in their psyche, something that would give them new life and energy. What they lack is not more gifts, but more conversion; they need a deeper relation with the source of life and energy.

The third reason that we find joy in the use of our gifts has to do with the realization of our deepest hope and longing. When Jesus came, all his work of teaching, preaching, and healing, all the miracles, everything that he did in his earthly ministry was related to the kingdom of God. He described that reign in healings and in parables, he called people to become part of God's reign, and he confronted them in an unavoidable way with their decision for or against God's rule. The reign of God is a new thing brought by God into this world, a transformation which makes all things new. The contrast with the present world is shown by the difficulty we have in describing God's reign with anything but negatives: it will be a time in which there is no sorrow, no sadness, no hunger, no war, no poverty, no loneliness, no oppression or injustice. But the reality of it will far transcend our ability to describe it merely in negative terms. It will be truth, rightness, justice, love revealed in power and fullness rather than haltingly, in hints and glimpses, as it is now. The coming of God's reign will show us the shallowness of our concrete hopes, and will at the same time fulfill our deepest hopes and dreams. It will bring into being what we would have hoped for had we had the courage.

The catechism of the Episcopal Church also asks: *What is the mission of the Church?* It answers: *The mission of the Church is to restore all people to unity with God and each other in Christ.*

The mission of the church is the mission of Christ, the reign of God. Only the church is given this mission, and it is the Church's only mission. When I write of "God's cause," this is the one I mean.

The catechism's statement of mission is not quite complete, for our call is not to restore only the people to unity, but all of creation; the stories of Genesis are particularly emphatic in stating that the animals are included in creation, and so a biblical understanding of creation sees that the natural order is so tightly related to the human order that one cannot be restored without the other.

This is a quibble, however, and the catechism statement of mission admirably reminds us of our first priority. All our church programs, all our spiritual paths and skillful means, all our activity on behalf of God, may be evaluated by this one statement: does it contribute to the restoration?

There is something about the ministry of reconciliation that goes together with gifts. We were and are created to live in a reconciled and restored world, not in the broken and disordered world we inhabit. Our abilities to imagine and co-recreate that world are built into us at the deepest, most primitive and archetypal level. Therefore the use of our gifts can give the kind of primitive joy that other primitive pleasures do—sex, running, eating. When we use our spiritual gifts, we are touching some of the deepest parts of our being, the place where we are most closely connected to God.

Using our gifts in doing God's work is a way of acting toward and on behalf of that which we hope and long for in our heart of hearts. It is a way of affirming my best self, my self as it was created to be, and of acting on my deepest values. At times we use our gifts effectively, to achieve a realistic outcome. At other times we use them to do something which is crazy or futile by worldly standards, but which is an eschatological symbol, a way of affirming our hope and of calling the world to turn to the future reign of God as Jesus himself did: "Repent and be saved, for the kingdom of God is at hand!"

If we believe in the coming reign of God, then when we act toward it and on its behalf, we are also affirming and acting on our deepest values. It cannot be otherwise than joyful, even though it involves conflict or pain. If we want to believe in God's reign, acting toward it and on its behalf is a way of choosing intentionally what we want and value in life, of discovering and refining and shaping our images of the reign so that we may act more authentically and effectively on its behalf.

The third question to which the answer is "spiritual gifts" is: What is a Christian response to the New Age movement?

One tradition of thought in the West has always attempted to see the world whole, as wholly created by and wholly related to God. This viewpoint bestowed a comforting unity in the past which we have not enjoyed in modern times; lacking it, we pay a certain price. One of the ironies of modern times is the scramble in physics for a unified theory of matter, sometimes called a Theory of Everything; one senses a certain longing for the same kind of unity of viewpoint which characterized the great medieval synthesis. Yet this effort on the part of physicists is based on a discipline which is not comprehensive enough in scope to yield more than a partial and therefore failed unification.

The second tradition is that of the Enlightenment, a rationalism which may be described as the attempt to see the world without reference to God. It may be said to have truly begun with the remark of the French mathematician Pierre Simon de Laplace (1749–1827) upon the presentation of his great work on celestial mechanics to his patron Napoleon Bonaparte. Napoleon remarked that Laplace's book did not contain a single reference to God, whereon Laplace replied, "Sire, I have no need of that hypothesis."

These two traditions of thought have often been in conflict, less often in harmony. Each owes to the other more than it has ever acknowledged. The existence of the two traditions side-by-side is reflected in the existence of parallel institutions in many areas of life: spiritual guidance and psychotherapy, the church as benefactor of the poor alongside government and private welfare institutions, the seminary alongside the university, religious private schools alongside public secular schools, and so on. Among these parallel movements may be numbered the spiritual discipline and lore of spiritual gifts on the one hand, and on the other the assortment of therapies and attitudes which have personal growth or the development of human potential as their goal and are lumped under the broad term "New Age movement". This movement is in part an outgrowth of the human potential movement of the sixties, and continues its emphasis on developing the ability of the individual to meet his or her own needs.

The existence of the New Age and similar movements is a judgment on the church's inability to provide a sense of human dignity, nobility, or worth to individuals. An over-emphasis on God's transcendence and goodness, and therefore on human limitation and sinfulness, seemed to make being human not worthwhile. The New Age movement at its best has given humanity a sense of capability, of competence, even of grandeur, which is to be welcomed, whatever the limitations of the movement itself. In some respects it has made valuable contributions to our life on this planet and to our perception of ourselves as able, worthwhile beings. It is not my purpose to denigrate or even to catalog the limitations of the movement, save to mention one which is important to a discussion of spiritual gifts. The movement has no sense of purpose outside itself, no context in which our newly-discovered potential should be exercised. My persistent questioning of friends who are in the movement took place along these lines: "But what are these potentials good for? When you've discovered and developed them, what then? Do you talk about helping others, about love, justice, peace —what? Certainly you can act so as to get your needs met— but do you really know what you need most? And what then—is getting your needs met all there is to life?" Usually there had been no thought given to the purpose and context for the use of the newly-discovered potential; it was seen as worthwhile in and of itself, with no other context or justification needed. When some thought had been given to this question—the answer was most often something like "to help others" or "to save the earth"—those in the New Age movement were not able to relate what they were doing to anything concrete that might be helpful to others.

From my point of view, the discovery and use of one's spiritual gifts combines the exciting self-discovery of human potential with the opportunity to use that potential or gift in the service of the renewal of the world through God's action in bringing God's reign fully into being.

There are other questions about spiritual gifts which are commonly asked. One such question is: what is the difference between spiritual gifts and human talents?

The difference between spiritual gifts and human talents may be stated in a single word: conversion. By conversion I mean the process of taking on the mind of Christ, of seeing the world more and more as God's creation, of giving up more and more of what blocks us from relationship with God, and of taking on more and more what joins us to God. Thus the difference between spiritual gifts and natural talents does not lie in the abilities that the different words describe, but the viewpoint and intentionality of the possessor and user of the abilities. If I see the world as God's creation, the place where God is acting to create and redeem the world, if I see myself and my abilities as a part of that creation, and if I choose and will to follow God's invitation to me to join in this work, then I am using my abilities in God's service— they are spiritual gifts. If I think of my own abilities as natural talents and use them for self-gratification or for altruism, then they are simply human talents. But because I see them as different and put them to different use, that does not make them different.

Another often-asked question is this one: Is there a level of spiritual development that must be attained before discovering and using spiritual gifts is appropriate, a "readiness" for gifts similar to readiness for mathematical thinking or reading?

While I believe that the discovery and use of spiritual gifts is appropriate at any stage of spiritual development, it seems that the work of discovering and using one's gifts is more fruitful and more natural if certain preliminaries are in place. It is helpful if one feels secure as part of a community of faith and has had some good experience in that community. There is a sense in which faith is the faith of the community before it can be appropriated by an individual, and so a certain amount of incorporation into the community seems to be desirable, perhaps even necessary.

If that has occurred, then there often comes a time when the person-in-community begins to question the community values and traditions and to begin to shape a more personal faith. This is what John Westerhoff describes in his book *Will Our Children Have Faith?* as "searching faith"; psychologically, it marks the beginning of the individual's differentiation from the rest of the community. This seems a most opportune time to learn one's spiritual gifts, for our gifts mark our uniqueness at the same time that they confirm that we are claimed and blessed by God.

There are other important questions about spiritual gifts, and each of these will receive a chapter-length discussion. What can we learn from Scripture about spiritual gifts? How can I find my own spiritual gifts? How do I know what to do with my spiritual gifts once I have found them? What is the church's role in helping people to discover and use their gifts? What do spiritual gifts have to do with traditional spiritual paths? And how can I help others to find and use their gifts?

In his book *Wishful Thinking*, Frederick Buechner writes, "The place God calls you to is the place where your deep gladness and the world's deep hunger meet." Our task in the rest of this book is to find the places of our deep gladness and of the world's deep hunger, and to reflect on God's call to us at the meeting of the two.

SPIRITUAL GIFTS IN CHRISTIAN TRADITION

The primary source for information about spiritual gifts is the New Testament, especially the Epistles to the Romans and the Ephesians and the First Epistle to the Corinthians. Much of our understanding of spiritual gifts comes from these passages. In this chapter we will look at these passages to learn what was taught or assumed in the New Testament church about spiritual gifts.

As the New Testament church grew, it developed institutions—theological, liturgical, and credal—to meet its needs. After the New Testament reached its final form, the institutions continued to develop to meet the changing needs of the church and of the culture. Many of the institutions underwent major changes after the completion of the form of the New Testament. Understanding these changes is especially important for understanding why interest in spiritual gifts all but disappeared soon after the New Testament period. We will look at some of these changes in the church and at their influence on the attitudes toward ministry that the New Testament writings assumed.

Scripture also gives us some ways of thinking about answers to some of the important questions about spiritual gifts. We will look at one such question, the difference between spiritual gifts and natural talents, in the context of what Scripture has to say about stewardship.

Finally, we will consider how, in the light of this tradition, we may profitably understand such gifts today.

Spiritual Gifts in the New Testament

The term "gift" is used many times in Holy Scripture, and it is used in two ways. Generally speaking it refers to any kind of gift, and may be summarized in these two statements,

"Every good endowment and every perfect gift is from
above. . . " (James 1:17) and the primary gift of God is the
Holy Spirit. All gifts are from God, and the greatest one, from
whom all others flow, is the Holy Spirit.

The second and more specific use of the term "gift" refers
to what are called spiritual gifts. Even here the terminology
is a little misleading, for only in Romans 1:11 is the term
"spiritual gifts" used. I prefer the term "gifts for ministry,"
for that is their purpose, but "gifts for ministry" is not a
biblical term. "Gift" in this sense refers to the ability of an
individual to perform particular acts of ministry—healing,
teaching, preaching, for example—which are needed by the
church for its mission. There are many gifts, and different
ones are given to different persons. I Peter provides an
example and summary of this use of the term: "As each has
received a gift, employ it for one another, as good stewards
of God's varied grace: whoever speaks, as one who utters
oracles of God; whoever renders service, as one who renders
it by the strength which God supplies; in order that in
everything God might be glorified through Jesus Christ" (I
Peter 4:10). Spiritual gifts are preeminently about "God's
varied grace," about the various ways that grace is given to
individuals and through them to the communities of faith to
which they belong, and about the stewardship of that grace.

There are three major references to spiritual gifts in the
New Testament: Romans 12, I Corinthians 12, and Ephesians
4. In addition to these, there are many passing references to
"gifts", and it is often a matter of interpretation as to whether
these passing references refer to spiritual gifts or more
generally to any kind of gifts. In this section we will look at
the major passages in some detail, and will also look at
several of the passing references to see what we can learn
from them.

But these passages, which refer either to explicit spiritual
gifts or to gifts in general, do not tell the whole story. Earlier
I said that the difference between spiritual gifts and natural

talents lay in the degree of conversion of the one who possesses them. To have a complete picture of spiritual gifts in the New Testament church, it is necessary to read also some of the passages which tell of how the converted use the resources they have. I will not look at these passages in detail, but will rather carry out the discussion in this chapter against a background of biblical understanding of stewardship.

Let us begin with the three classic passages in the New Testament. They are Romans 12, verses 4–8; I Corinthians 12, verses 4 through 11 (with Paul's additional discussion in verses 12–31 and also 14:1–19); and Ephesians 4, verses 11–12, with further comments in verses 1–7 and 13–16. Consider first the passage in Romans:

> For as in one body we have many members, and all the members do not have the same function, so we, though many, are one body in Christ, and individually members one of another. Having gifts that differ according to the grace given to us let us use them: if prophecy, in proportion to our faith; if service, in our serving; he who teaches, in his teaching; he who exhorts, in his exhortation; he who contributes, in liberality; he who gives aid, with zeal; he who does acts of mercy, with cheerfulness.

This epistle, in which he introduces himself to the church at Rome and gives a coherent account of his teaching, is the most systematic of Paul's writings. After laying out the great theological themes of the first eleven chapters, Paul turns in chapter 12 to exhortation, encouragement in right living. He is writing, in effect, "In the light of what I have written about God's graceful actions in the first eleven chapters, do this!" Paul begins chapter 12 with an exhortation to ". . . worship . . . by offering your living bodies as a holy sacrifice, truly pleasing to God. Do not model yourselves on the behavior of the world around you . . .". Then, as an example of not conforming to the world, he urges his reader not to exaggerate his real importance. He uses the analogy of his readers' union with Christ to a human body, in which each part has a separate function. As we are members of Christ, so we belong to each other.

"Our gifts differ," he writes, "according to the grace given us. If your gift is prophecy, then use it as your faith suggests; if administration, then use it for administration; if teaching, then use it for teaching. Let the preachers deliver sermons, the almsgivers give freely, the officials be diligent, and those who do works of mercy do them cheerfully." Then Paul moves on to the importance of love, hope, hospitality, and perseverance.

We see several themes in this brief passage. First is humility—having an accurate, down-to-earth knowledge of the self and its importance. We are important because we have been given particular grace (note that Paul is not writing about an *amount* of grace, but about a *dimension* of grace, the dimension having to do with the particular gift). No one is to think more highly of himself than he ought, but on the other hand no one is to fail to use her gift. Paul evidently did not think it necessary to warn against thinking *less* of oneself than one ought; today that is a necessary exhortation. But he does encourage people to use the gifts they have been given for what they were given for. That this encouragement was necessary at all makes Paul's exhortation sound very modern!

Second is the image of the body. We are important because we are joined together with Christ as the parts of a human body are joined together. In each of the major writings about gifts, the image of the body is used in the same way. In each of the places where Paul mentions gifts of the spirit, he links his discussion to the body of Christ. What is the body? It is the fellowship of those people, no matter who or where they are, who (in Hans Kung's useful phrase) serve "the cause of God." They may belong to a church or not; they may consider themselves Christians or not. But they recognize one another by their common allegiance to God and to God's reign.

Paul's message here is that the gifts are given so that the cause of God might be served. Each person is given at least one gift. They are to use them in ways complementary to one another, and they are to honor one another's gift and not to regard their own gift more highly than another's. A similar image is that of a well-equipped concert orchestra, in which each instrument has its distinctive part and all are needed for harmony.

Finally, Paul lists representative gifts and roles: prophecy, administration, teaching, preaching, almsgiving, officiating, and doing works of mercy. Each person is to use her gift as she is given it, and to use it with faith and in good cheer. Note that even in this most systematic of Paul's writings, he never gives a definitive list of spiritual gifts. The lists of gifts in Paul's writings differ somewhat from each other. Paul seems to assume that his readers are familiar with the various gifts and that it is therefore not necessary to define them or to list them carefully.

We look now at the passage in I Corinthians.

Now there are varieties of gifts, but the same Spirit; and there are varieties of service, but the same Lord; and there are varieties of working, but it is the same God who inspires them all in every one. To each is given the manifestation of the Spirit for the common good. To one is given through the Spirit the utterance of wisdom, and to another the utterance of knowledge according to the same Spirit, to another faith by the same Spirit, to another gifts of healing by the one Spirit, to another the working of miracles, to another prophecy, to another the ability to distinguish between spirits, to another various kinds of tongues, to another the interpretation of tongues. All these are inspired by one and the same Spirit, who apportions to each one individually as he wills.

The situation in which this was written was quite different from that of Romans, and the tone and content of this letter reflect the difference. Here Paul is writing topically about two sets of concerns: first, what he has heard about the Corinthian church, and second, what the Corinthians themselves have asked him about in their letter(s) to him. Paul has heard, first, that there has been "division" among them, division based on factions who variously claim to follow Christ, Apollo, and Paul. He has heard that some of them believe themselves to be more "spiritual" than others because they are able to have ecstatic experiences. These "spiritual" ones believe that these experiences are sufficient for their faith, and that they do not need the discipline of love. Furthermore, we gather that the Corinthians do not believe in an actual resurrection of the dead, but are talking about a "spiritual" resurrection of some kind.

Paul's writing about gifts is part of his vigorous polemic to this congregation, and his message in this section is that no one of the gifts is to be regarded as greater than the others, nor is the bearer to lord it over the others on the basis of a supposed superiority.

A third theme in Paul's writing about gifts is the unity of the body of Christ. The primary gift, here as elsewhere, is the gift of the Holy Spirit. As it is a spirit of unity, so is the church to be one in spirit. It is natural for Paul to write about the body in the letter to the church at Corinth, and that he link it to his discussion of gifts. For one of the reasons for this letter was the Corinthians' use of the gifts of the spirit as a pretext for dividing the congregation into "first-class" and "second-class" Christians. Paul emphasizes here as in Romans that the gifts (and their bearers) are not to be ranked in that way, and that the gifts are not to be used for the purpose of dividing the body.

I believe that we may take this as license for using the broadest latitude in searching for our gifts. For if they are to be used in the service of God, and if the specific details of God's cause change in each age (though not its overall direction), then we may be sure of being given, as a community of faith, all the gifts we need in whatever proportion they are required by the specific nature of God's cause in every age. If God's cause requires persons with the gift of evangelism, we will have persons with that gift. But if it requires persons with the gifts required to research alternatives to nuclear weapons, we will also have persons with that gift. If it requires Christians with a gift for peacemaking, they too will be part of the community.

One verse in I Corinthians merits particular attention because it has been the subject of considerable controversy. In the 31st verse of chapter 12, Paul writes: "Be ambitious for the higher gifts." This has often been understood to mean that there is a hierarchy of gifts, with some gifts more important, or higher, than the others. These higher gifts have been taken to be the word-oriented gifts, such as preaching, teaching, and prophecy. This verse has been linked with the reference in Romans to "spiritual gifts", and it has been written that these word-oriented gifts are the spiritual gifts, and are to be sought most vigorously.[1]

I would disagree with this understanding for several reasons. First, the idea that there is a hierarchy of gifts goes directly counter to what Paul has so vigorously defended for the past thirty verses, namely that there is no hierarchy, that all the gifts are important, and that people are not to make distinctions on the basis of such a hierarchy. Second, the terms "spiritual" and "gift" are used together in only one place, namely, in Romans 1:11. It is not clear that Paul is using "spiritual" to distinguish from other, "non-spiritual" gifts. To assume that he is using it in this way and then to link the assumed distinction with the various lists of gifts in I Corinthians, an epistle written some years earlier, seems to me to be straining for an interpretation.

It seems that in writing about the "higher gifts" Paul is making the transition to the next chapter, on love, and is encouraging his readers to seek the great gifts of God, such as faith, hope, and love, and not to be so concerned with the

particular gift they have been given and with their status in
the community based on their gift and its value.

Finally, we look at the passage in Ephesians on the gifts
of the Spirit.

> There is one body and one Spirit, just as you were called
> to the one hope that belongs to your call, one Lord, one
> faith, one baptism, one God and Father of us all, who is
> above all and through all and in all. But grace was given
> to each of us according to the measure of Christ's gift. . . .

> And his gifts were that some should be apostles, some
> prophets, some evangelists, some pastors and teachers, to
> equip the saints for the work of ministry, for building up
> the body of Christ, until we all attain to the unity of the
> faith and of the knowledge of the Son of God, to mature
> manhood, to the measure of the stature of the fulness of
> Christ. . .

> We are to grow up in every way into him who is the
> head, into Christ, from whom the whole body, joined and
> knit together by every joint with which it is supplied, when
> each part is working properly, makes bodily growth and
> upbuilds itself in love.

The themes are by now familiar. It urges unity in the Spirit,
on the basis of the unity of Lord, faith, baptism, and of the
one God who is Father of all, "over all, through all and within
all." But unity of the body does not mean identity of its
members, for the author concludes with the observation that
each of us has been given our own share of grace. We may
infer from the context that he does not mean "share" in a
quantitative sense; he means not more nor less grace, but
different gifts. The building of the kingdom of God requires
many different gifts and the body has been given all it needs
for its task.

Why are we given gifts? "So that the saints together make
a unity in the work of service, building up the body of Christ.
In this way we are all to come to unity in our faith and in our

knowledge of the Son of God, until we become the perfect Man, fully mature with the fullness of Christ himself" (Ephesians 4:12-13). Through our use of our gifts in service to others, we ourselves reach maturity, and the body of Christ is built up and unified, made whole. In verses 15 and 16 Ephesians uses the image of the body, now with Christ as the head "by whom the whole body is fitted and joined together, every joint adding its own strength, for each separate part to work according to its function. So the body grows until it has built itself up, in love."

In summary, these three passages paint a picture of the church as a community of persons who are called to grow in unity with one another by serving one another, each one using his or her gift and each one valuing the gifts of others. Paul's continuing concern with unity and his strong language early in I Corinthians discloses a particular lack of unity in that congregation, but a call to unity is clearly present in all three passages.

One question which arises naturally at this point is: why is there no mention of spiritual gifts in any of the four gospels? Why are they mentioned only in other writings? Are gifts peripheral to the gospel of Christ, or are they close to the .center of the gospel? How important are they to authentic life in Christ?

I believe that an answer may be given along several lines. First, the idea of gifts is not *contrary* to anything in the' gospels; they are at least consistent with one another, and the use of gifts fits quite naturally with the gospel description of life in Christ as service to others. Second, Paul's purpose in writing the epistles was quite different from that of the Gospel writers. Paul's are occasional letters. They respond to the practical questions and needs of these congregations. Even in Romans, Paul's "summa," his concerns are very much the same as in the other epistles; his characteristic concerns are written in every line. They are practical concerns, and the spiritual gifts are quite practically ways to live the life in Christ in service to others. The gospel writers, on the other hand, had less immediate goals in mind. They were giving a story, a world view, a perspective on the world which allowed for the New Being which God was bringing about; if they spent less time on the particular problems of life in Christ, it is because they spent more time on their primary purpose of telling the story in ways in which their hearers could participate.

Finally, the few specific references to gifts in the later books of Scripture, such as I Peter and Hebrews, imply that gifts were widely understood and were simply assumed by the church of those periods. One doesn't write in detail about what everyone knows and assumes; one refers to it, as these later authors do, and moves on. Because the cultural distance between I Corinthians and, say, Hebrews, is so great, one may conjecture with some confidence that the knowledge of gifts was widespread and assumed in the early church.

From Cult to Church

As reflected in the texts above, the boundaries of the New Testament church were pretty well defined. It was clear who was in and who was not in. The lengthy preparation for Holy Baptism made everyone aware of who had participated in that sacrament and who had not. Partly due to the occasional danger, partly due to the social and official disapproval of Christians, partly due to the lengthy period of preparation, the boundaries were clearly drawn.

Along with the clear boundaries went a certain fluidity of roles. Everyone was expected to do what he or she could. Specialization of ministry was more on the basis of gifts, less on the basis of role. Even worship was relatively "flexible", with "a psalm, hymn, or spiritual song" offered by whomever had one.[2] The early church as well-defined as to boundary, but it lacked much of a hierarchy.[3]

The church of that late New Testament period was an alternative community, alternative to the social structures of the world. Depending on the era, the church was more or less an immediate eschatological community, living in daily expectation of the world's end, but it always existed apart from the culture. It tried to live a communal life based on unity in the Spirit rather than on cultural status and boundaries. It tried to live as a community of reconciliation rather than as a cultural community of control, status, and alienation. It was more an alternative to the culture than a counter-cultural movement.

All these characteristics changed within a few centuries of the writing of the New Testament books.

Because of the threat from teachers of false doctrines, the early church went on to erect a structure of control and authority which would ensure the teaching of correct doctrine and the passage of correct doctrine from one generation to the other. This it did with the establishment of the creeds, the orders of ministry, and the canon of scripture. The creeds provided a summary of beliefs which were useful for catechesis and which could also serve as a test of orthodoxy. The orders of ministry, especially the historic episcopate, were intended to ensure the continuity of accurate doctrine from one generation to the next. And the canon of scripture was intended to ensure that heterodox writings would not be passed off as orthodox. Thus the skeleton, the administrative structure, which was largely lacking in the church of the texts cited above, was put in place under the pressures of the age.

This happened just in time, for the boundaries of the church quickly dissolved. The Constantinian settlement of the early fourth century provided social acceptability for Christians, and later in the century required that one be a Christian to hold public office. This gave the church safety and respectability, but also opened its doors to those with questionable motivations for membership. The possibility of even minimal catechesis was gone, and so the church became a victim of its numbers.

In view of the numbers of relatively uncatechized people in the post-Constantinian church, the question arose: Who was to perform the necessary functions of the church, such as leadership in liturgy and teaching? The answer was, "The ordained." They had some training and they were more or less accountable to the local bishop. So the backbone which was put in place within the first four centuries did not involve the average person, but was used primarily to maintain lines of authority among ordained persons.

Along with the erosion of the boundary-skin and the building of the backbone, the nature and purpose of the church changed greatly in the first few centuries. To a great extent, this change was demanded by the changes in skin and backbone. With the erosion of the skin, it was no longer possible to maintain the idea of the church as alternative community; rather, the church tended to become one with the culture. It lost the distance necessary to speak prophetically to the culture, and became largely a legitimizer of cultural institutions. The age of Christendom (as distinct from Christianity) had set in.

The effect on the ideas about and use of spiritual gifts was dramatic. No longer was everyone encouraged to use whatever gifts they possessed; now the ministry was increasingly in the hands of the ordained, who, if the question of gifts arose at all, were implicitly expected to possess them. The degrees of ordained ministry increased to encompass all the functions of ministry, until by medieval times even the role of doorkeeper required ordination. The people were regarded as passive recipients of ministry; little training or enabling of their ministry was offered them and less was expected of them. Despite some notable lay movements, this attitude persisted with little substantive variation until this century; in fact, the modern notion of professional ordained ministry, with all the expectations expressed in the word "professional", has carried this attitude to an extreme.

Spiritual Gifts or Natural Talents?
What is the difference between spiritual gifts and natural talents? This question is best understood in the context of stewardship, the wise and faithful use of what we have received, and we will do that in this section. But first it is worthwhile to clarify the question. A major source of confusion is the ambiguity of the term "spiritual". It is commonly used with many different meanings, and many of the meanings are not helpful to a clear understanding of spiritual gifts. Let us look at some ways in which this term is used.

One way of clarifying the term is to ask, "What is its opposite? From what is it differentiated?" For those in an esoteric or metaphysical tradition, "spiritual" often means "non-physical". They might cite the text from John 4:24, "God is spirit." So for them the question becomes, "Which gifts are spiritual and which are physical?" The physical ones might be looks, height, strength or agility or physical gracefulness; the spiritual ones would be intangibles such as intelligence or compassion.

Another way to understand the question is to oppose "spiritual" to "worldly". Now the non-spiritual gifts are those I can use to make a living, to survive, while the spiritual gifts become somehow unworldly, impractical, useless for survival. The former are essential, the latter optional. The former are somehow substantial, while the latter, unrelated to the necessities of life, finally are insubstantial. Somehow this understanding of the question is itself worldly; "spiritual" means unimportant, unreal. We are only slightly removed from the previous understanding, where "real" meant "physical". Now "real" means "practical".

Under either of these understandings, the question assumes that it is possible to divide the list of gifts in two: spiritual and not-spiritual. A look at two events in the life and death of Jesus should show the impossibility of this, and may lead to a better understanding of the question.

Some Pharisees approach Jesus, trying to trap him. "Should we pay the tax to Caesar, or not?" they ask. To refuse to pay would align Jesus with the Zealots, the violent anti-Roman faction, while paying the tax would acknowledge the authority of the hated Roman Empire. Jesus' response is to hold up a Roman coin. "Whose image does this coin bear?" he asks, and they answer, "Caesar's." (Mark 12:13-17 and parallels in Matthew 22:15-22 and Luke 20:20-26)

Now the term "image" has a long and distinguished tradition in Judaism. According to the second Genesis account of creation, God created humankind in his own image, "male and female he created them." The second commandment forbids the making of graven images. Why? Because they distract us from looking upon that first image, "the face of God in the face of man" (Rabbi Heschel). So when Jesus held up the Roman coin and used the term "image", he was challenging their trick question with its false antitheses and was raising for them a profound question. "If you are concerned about who owns this coin that bears Caesar's image," he was saying in effect, "how much more should you be concerned about who owns you, you who bear the image of God himself! And if God owns you, does God not own everything about you, including your natural abilities?"

For Christians, the term "spiritual" does not mean "non-physical" or "not-practical", but rather "related to God". For Paul, "spiritual gifts" meant "gifts from God". Therefore the question "What is the difference between spiritual gifts and natural talents?" is not the same as asking, "How can I divide my gifts into two lists, spiritual and non-spiritual?" Rather, it is to ask "Do I belong to God—completely, with every gift that I have been given? Am I not made for God's service, made to use everything I have for God's full reign?" When Jesus says,"Render to Caesar what is Caesar's and to God what is God's", he challenges his listeners—and us—to ask,

"What is not God's? And am I not God's own? And if I am God's, is not everything of mine also God's, all that I am and have, including my gifts?"

Another scene from Jesus's life and death: Jesus dying on the cross. At the hour of his death, the veil of the temple was torn. No more was the Holy of Holies protected from the gaze of the curious. There was no wall between God and humanity. The law, which had divided the world into clean and unclean, holy and worldly, was fulfilled; God had entered the world. It is no longer possible to divide the world, or any part of the world, into two inventory lists, holy and worldly, sacred and profane, clean and unclean. The world is God's, all of it. God reigns over all, "drawing all things together in Christ."

Buried somehow in our original question, "Which gifts are spiritual and which are not?", there is potentially a plea: "What can I withhold from God's service? What can I claim as my own, for my own use and welfare, accountable to no one for its stewardship?"

Jesus' answer might be, "Whatever you need to, for now. But don't forget that it all belongs to God, and is given to you for use on his behalf, whether you choose to offer it or not."

We have seen what changes have taken place across the centuries in our understanding of spiritual gifts. Now it is time to suggest ways in which we might fruitfully view them today. I suggest that there are four ideas which might stand as guides in our present-day understanding of gifts.

First, gifts are for the reconciliation of the world. They are for use in the cause of God, for bringing reconciliation and healing, love and truth and justice, the divine reign of right relationships with each other and with God.

Second, my gifts are given to complement the gifts of others. This implies that part of my growth into the wise and faithful use of my gifts must be learning to let others use theirs in ways complementary to my use of mine. I need to learn the art of cooperation in the cause of God. This implies that the locus of discovering and claiming and using and reflecting on the use of my gifts is the community of faith. To practice cooperation in the use of gifts is to be in community; in fact, "community" in its root meaning has to do with doing things together.

This theme implies an alternative to any hierarchical view of the community of faith, the church. Whoever has the gift of administration is the administrator, not who has the greatest desire or the most power. In particular, the ordained persons are not expected to have more gifts than others. A view of gifts which stresses cooperation and community is one in which every person has his or her ministry, but in which each person's ministry is seen as part of the whole ministry of the church.

The most exciting and hopeful prospect for the kingdom of God is, I believe, the discovery that all the members of the church are important to its realization. Without this discovery, the ideas of spiritual gifts would be considerably less important. The church could then be seen as a mere institution, with tasks assigned based on institutional roles, with power granted on the basis of place in the hierarchy, and with place in the hierarchy guaranteed by one's level of ordination, one's institutional title. But the inevitable tendency of institutions is towards idolatry—to promote their own welfare and to lay claim to status. Therefore the church must also be seen as something other than institution—as family of God, as Spirit-filled body. While it is necessary in our time that the church be an institution, it is also true that where the church is understood only as institution the kingdom of God is forgotten or subverted. The discovery of the ministry of all the people of the church may help us to maintain alternate understandings of the church, understandings which promote the kingdom of God. To do this, we must find more ways of valuing people's ministries that are based on their gifts and not on their status. The institution cannot assign value without somehow formalizing or setting it in stone, thereby running the risk of subverting it; it must be done informally by all the people of the church.

The catechism of the Episcopal Church asks: *What is the ministry of the laity?* and answers: *The ministry of lay persons is to represent Christ and his Church; to bear witness to him wherever they may be; and, according to the gifts given them, to carry on Christ's work of reconciliation in the world; and to take their place in the life, worship, and governance of the Church.*[4]

This is a key statement for our understanding of gifts, for it mentions gifts in only one of the four aspects of the ministry of the laity. This raises several questions for us: Are we not to use our gifts in the other areas of our ministry, such as representing Christ and his church? What is there about Christ's work of reconciliation in the world which is specially concerned with the use of gifts?

This passage can well serve as a reminder that the use of our gifts is not the whole of our ministry as lay persons. There are some things that come first and that may not require the use of our spiritual gifts. For example, representing Christ and his church in the world requires awareness, courage and faithfulness first and may require spiritual gifts, but no one can avoid this part of the ministry by saying "I don't have those gifts." Similarly, taking one's place in the life, worship, and governance of the church may require the use of one's gifts, but there are times when work needs to be done and the appropriate gifts are not available; then we do the work without the joy of using our gifts.

The first two themes imply a third: that the church is the place for discovering and claiming our gifts, but the world is the primary place for using them. In saying this, I don't have in mind a clear theological division between the church and the world. They are quite mixed together, in much the same way that, by God's grace, I am both human and divine. My point is a more mundane one, that we are called where there is brokenness in the world, and the work of the church is to pray and work for the healing of that brokenness. This may on occasion be within the body of Christ, but that is not the norm. The work of the church is not mainly "church work."

Gordon Cosby, pastor of the Church of the Savior in Washington, D.C., has written that the work of the church is to call forth the gifts of its members. The work of the church is not primarily good liturgy, or effective social action, or compassionate outreach, important as those are. They come and go, and the results are so often disappointing when viewed by the standards of effectiveness. When viewed as eschatological signs, events which give hope through a foretaste of the full reign of God, however, they are often more powerful than they otherwise appear. But the discovery of one's own gifts, and the results of support and encouragement in using them, lasts; the witness of someone using their gifts calls forth the gifts of another. "We are not sent out into the world in order to make people good," writes Cosby.

> We are not sent out to encourage them to do their duty. The reason people have resisted the Gospel is that we have gone out to make people good, to help them do their duty, to impose new burdens on them, rather than calling forth the gift which is the essence of the person himself. . . We begin by exercising our own gifts. The person who is having the time of his life doing what he is doing has a way of calling forth the deeps of another. Such a person is Good News. He is not *saying* the Good News. He *is* the Good News. He is the embodiment of the freedom of the new humanity. The person who exercises his own gifts in freedom can allow the Holy Spirit to do in others what He wants to do.[5]

This is a new way of looking at our Christian vocation, a way of looking not at what we are called to do, but at who we are called to be. So often our attempts to do good fall far short of success, and they are tempered by the realization that they are always, in some measure, self-serving. But the use of our gifts calls us to a new way of being, a way which does not deny or avoid our giftedness but rather claims and celebrates it. Frederick Buechner's words on vocation make the distinction:

> There are all different kinds of voices calling you to all different kinds of work, and the problem is to find out which is the voice of God rather than of Society, say, or the Superego, or Self-interest.
>
> By and large a good rule for finding out is this. The kind of work God usually calls you to is the kind of work (a) that you need most to do and (b) that the world most needs to have done. If you really get a kick out of your work you've presumably met requirement (a), but if your work is writing TV deodorant commercials, the chances are you've missed requirement (b). On the other hand, if your work is being a doctor in a leper colony, you've probably met requirement (b), but if most of the time you're bored and depressed by it, the chances are you have not only bypassed (a) but probably aren't helping your patients much either.[6]

It is so often difficult to know what kind of help a needy person needs. The helper is not always the best judge of what is needed, and the person who needs help is often not a good judge either. I believe that the idea of "helping people" describes well one part of the call to Christian ministry, but that it is far from a complete description. In ministry, we begin, as always, with thanksgiving for our gifts, and with the joy of using our gifts wherever they are appropriate. When we use ours, others find themselves using theirs, and they find that they have been helped without our setting out to help them. Jesus never described his ministry or anyone else's in such broad terms as "helping others"; he simply used his gifts in God's cause and left the outcome to God.

Therefore I would propose a fourth and final theme for the use of gifts in our time. Our task is not so much to "help" others as to be with them in their joy and sorrow. It is not so much to do for them as to be whole in their presence. It is not so much to save the world as to be the saved people that we are. For if life is preparation for the fully realized reign of God, then the test of our life is that when that reign arrives, we recognize it and welcome it, and we are prepared to live in it gladly and naturally, as true princes and princesses of the realm, sons and daughters of the King/Queen of creation. We prepare for it now by living as if it were fully present.

This calls for a renewed church, and a new way of understanding our vocation as the body of Christ. We are not out to save the world. God has done that, and Jesus's ministry, as characterized in the Gospel of John, was to dramatize and confront the world with the reality of eternal life and with the world's choice for or against it. That is our ministry also. Jesus dramatized and confronted the world by teaching, preaching and healing, and most of all by living each day in deep and filial relation with regard to God, and in freedom with regard to the world. He was an inviting person in his own gracefulness. We are called to live in the grace that comes with our world, with our life, and with our gifts, so that those about us may know the goodness of God by seeing what God has given us, and may be called into that same filial relation with God.

SPIRITUAL GIFTS TODAY

In the previous chapters we have looked at St. Paul's writings on spiritual gifts and then at their diminished value in succeeding centuries as the church became increasingly hierarchical and clericalized after the time of Constantine. Turning to the contemporary world, with its rediscovery of the significance of lay ministry in the churches, what do we see? What are some understandings of spiritual gifts today?

Seeing Gifts Through Smoke-Colored Glasses

For many Christians, the term "spiritual gifts" carries a negative connotation. It reminds them of shouting television evangelists who combine dramatic and suspect healings with dramatic and sentimental appeals for money. Or they may think of the early days of the charismatic movement in the mainline churches, when it seemed that the gift of speaking in tongues was the only one worth having and that those who didn't have it were somehow inadequate Christians. Or they may remember only the most notorious of the pentecostal experiences, such as the Jim Jones fiasco. Most Christians have not had a positive experience with spiritual gifts, and many have had negative ones.

If we ask if these negative images bear any relation to the right understanding of spiritual gifts of which Paul wrote, the answer is clearly "no." These negative ideas have much more to do with what Paul was writing *against*; they are misuses and misunderstandings of gifts. Today we find all the same abuses of gifts that Paul knew so well. We hear claims of superiority based on particular gifts, gifts used for personal advancement, gifts used entirely outside the context of the body of Christ. We see healing, even legitimate physical healing, done for its own sake, unrelated to God's greater gift of faith and the transformation, through that faith, of God's people. We see glossolalia—speaking in tongues—and its interpretation accepted as God's word without reflection, testing, or discernment.

This points out anew the power of gifts. When we discern and use gifts we draw close to the mystery and power of God. The very quality of being touched by the Holy Spirit, which lifts spiritual gifts out of the realm of the ordinary, also makes them suspect and open to abuse. It seems that one of the strategies of evil is to so mar the face of God's gift that we would see that gift as evil. We must not let our negative cultural images of these gifts turn us from recognizing them as legitimate gifts from a loving God, and from using them lovingly in God's cause.

Gifts for Lay Ministry

Even where there is no distrust of gifts themselves, many of our present ideas about clerical and lay ministry make it very difficult for both lay persons and clergy to discern and use their gifts.

Two recent conversations illustrate this difficulty. In the first, I spoke with a woman from another parish whose mother had been seriously ill. She said, "The thing that hurt most was that no one from the church came by to see her." Knowing that her mother was a life-long member of her parish and that most of her friends were also members, I asked her if they weren't "from the church." She said, "No, they came as my friends, not from the church."

A week later I had lunch with a friend who was the chairman of the pastoral care committee of another local parish. We talked of the number of gifted lay persons who are doing pastoral care alongside clergy in his parish, and of the excitement about lay ministry there. He remarked, "I used to think that clergy were people we hired to take our ministry away from us!"

The first conversation illustrates for me the widespread perception among lay persons that pastoral care received from other parishioners does not count. For this woman, if the clergy have not come, the church has not come. As for her friends, they consistently understood their ministry to her mother as being done out of friendship, with no reference to the call of Christ or to their common baptism or membership in the body of Christ. These attitudes support an over-clericalized idea of pastoring, which is not at all consistent with the picture of pastoral care in the early church that we find in Scripture. I am not arguing that laity should be the pastors instead of the clergy, but rather that lay pastoral ministry is equally valid and equally important; neither can replace the other. There are three essential sources for the ministry of pastoral care in the church, as for most other ministries: the ministry of the ordained; the ministry of gifted and designated lay persons; and the more informal but no less important ministries of the rest of the congregation. This vision of ministry requires changes in perception on the part of all Christians. They must begin to see themselves as people "ordained" at baptism as legitimate ministers of Christ, and, equally important, must learn to accept care from other lay persons, as well as from clergy, as if it were from Christ.

The second conversation illustrates for me the changing attitudes among some laity and some clergy toward a more complementary role for lay and clergy ministry. It is not so much that the clergy have taken away the ministry of the laity; rather, it has been in the short-term interest of both lay and clergy for clergy to do all the "official" ministry of the church. Generally speaking, in parish churches of the past few centuries, the clergy at their best ministered on behalf of the rest of the parish; at its worst, the laity of the parish allowed and depended on the clergy to minister in their stead. This tendency assumed that the clergy had all the gifts necessary for ministry and at the same time deprived the laity of a supportive environment in which to discover and use their own. All the gifts (to the extent that anyone thought in terms of using their gifts) were assumed to be confined to those in particular ordained roles; anyone else was believed presumptuous to think that they might have a ministry and the gifts to minister.

In the earlier books of the New Testament, the letters of Paul, ministry is seen more in terms of gifts than as specific roles in the community of faith; later, as in the later New Testament books such as I Peter, II Peter, and Jude, we see a movement toward making the functions of ministry into roles. Participation in shared ministry is, in many contemporary congregations, beginning to regain its proper balance. Following upon the highly visible liturgical ministries of lay readers and chalice bearers, the less visible pastoral lay ministries are also being reclaimed. Slowly, and with considerable resistance, the whole church is becoming more balanced. The pastoral ministry is but an example of a kind of ministry for which many are gifted but which has been limited to those in ordained roles. There are many other gifts for ministry which are being discovered and reclaimed, along with the authority for their use.

It is easy to think of gifts as merely useful "within the church" — used by members of the body of Christ on behalf of other members. We must continually remind ourselves that the purpose of the gifts is for the restoration of the world. All ministry is ultimately for that purpose. When most of the gifts of the members are used only within the parish, it has lost its balance in favor of introversion; it risks becoming ineffective in the world. A parish in which all the gifts of the members are used out in the world has lost its balance in favor of extraversion; it runs the risk of losing its energizing center of common life. All the gifts are necessary, all are important; but the purpose, the ultimate activity of the kingdom is in the world, not within the body.

The movement toward greater balance between lay and ordained ministry is not without its tensions. We are still young spiritually, much like the church at Corinth. It is inevitable that we will err in learning to use our gifts for ministry; where there is power there is the possibility of misuse. But we cannot turn away from the real gifts we have been given for God's work.

In chapter one we met Mary, Harrison, Al, Bill, Joan, Sam, and Heather. Each was in need of something—they did not know what. Mary felt her work, though enjoyable, was inadequate in meeting her need for meaning and purpose, while Harrison, about to retire from his job, wondered what he would be able to put in its place. Al, the research geologist, describes it this way: "I'm doing everything the church offers —if my need were spiritual, I'm sure I would have heard about it by now!" Bill, a high school senior, is drifting, unsure of his direction in life and struggling with parental pressure. Joan and Heather are both searching for some redeeming value in their experiences of suffering, Joan in her bout with depression and Heather in her struggles to survive her childhood with alcoholic parents. Sam's difficulty lies in what seems to him too many gifts and too many opportunities— how can he limit himself to one and ignore the rest?

Some of these wants and needs are simply part of being human. Others, however, might be satisfied by a knowledge of our individual gifts and a serious commitment to exploring and using them. Let's now imagine a parish that might provide each of these people with the resources he or she needs, a congregation in which the discovery and use of spiritual gifts plays a central role.

In a Gifted Parish

Such a parish is, first of all, a place to discover one's gifts —not once a year, but all year round. Gifts are talked about, preached about, taught about. It is not possible for a person to be a member of this parish without knowing about gifts and continually being confronted with the discovery and use of one's own gifts.

Mary is a long-time member of the parish. When she discovers that her childhood love for playing the piano has not left her, she signs up for lessons. Soon she is playing hymns, and volunteers to play piano for a Wednesday afternoon hymn-sing at a nearby nursing home. Over the next few months, Mary gets to know some of the people who live in the nursing home. They enjoy her playing and let her know it, and she realizes that her playing revives warm memories of her own mother's delight with her playing. She feels more connected with her mother and with her childhood, and regains some of the excitement, creativity, and happiness of her childhood. Her life seems to have a new dimension, a new unity. Her new enthusiasm and energy carries over into her work with speech-and-hearing impaired persons, and she approaches them with new creativity and depth.

Although a life-long member of another congregation, à quiet, traditional parish, Al finds his way to this same church through a friend who is a member, and who has told him of some of the exciting work there with gifts. Al visits and is surprised by the energy in the congregation. People are filled with purpose and seem, for the most part, to know what they are doing with their lives. He is also surprised by the great differences among members of the congregation, differences in economic status, race, and lifestyle, and by the way in which those differences are usually taken for granted. The members seem to accept conflicts as normal, able to disagree without holding on to their grudges. Al notices that when people do disagree they do it safely, without fear of reprisal, and that they do not "lose face" when a decision goes against them. In talking with his friend in the parish, he finds that differences are valued and expressed more openly than in other parishes he has visited, and that peoples' gifts are understood to be among the many expressions of their uniqueness.

Al also notices people in this congregation who are not interested in learning or using their gifts, and finds that they too are vitally involved in the life of the congregation. There is little exclusion of one portion of the congregation by another portion, even though they do not share this interest. Parishioners most caught up in learning about and using their gifts say that others are often using their gifts without being aware of it, and that there is plenty of work to go around.

After visiting for several months, Al finds that he is quite uncomfortable with this level of conflict and diversity in a church. It goes against his grain. After worshipping with his friend for six months, he returns to his old parish where things are quieter and more uniform. Yet Al does not relate his experience with this lively parish to the emptiness in his life.

Such a parish supports the exploration of new-found gifts. It understands that this is often tentative, and that people feel vulnerable and fragile as they do it. Alongside the ongoing program of gifts discovery, they need an environment— other individuals and small groups—where they can talk about their insights, about their successes and failures.

In his senior year in high school, Bill is dreading college. He is certainly academically able, even gifted, but the high and conflicting expectations which his parents place on his choice of college major are robbing him of the excitement and pleasure which he should be feeling toward his first year of college. He senses that much of their expectation is based on the fear that he will simply drift if they don't encourage him to do what they want. If he had an arguable alternative to propose, Bill thinks they would be open to letting him try it. But he doesn't — at least, nothing he could tell his parents about. He is aware that his lack of a specific direction is easily interpreted by his parents as "drifting."

Bill has heard about spiritual gifts through his church, but never in regard to himself or to the real world, either. He is occasionally active with the youth program of the church, mentioning one evening to a youth worker that he is thinking of not going to college because of the pressure that he is getting from his parents. The youth worker is sensitive, and understands that Bill is searching for a presentable alternative to college. So he tells Bill of gifts that he has observed in him, such as a good analytic mind, the fact that people come to him with problems and troubling situations because they find his comments helpful. However the youth worker does not tell Bill that gifts often have little to do with the work we have to do, and that Bill would be a fortunate person indeed if his work used his gifts well. He does arrange for Bill to take some vocational and personality tests at the career placement service of the local college. They show that one of the vocations he might be well suited for is psychology, with counselling as a specialty. Bill now has the information he needs to suggest an alternative to his parents.

Joan is nearing the end of a course of psychotherapy for her depression. She is feeling more optimistic, more energetic, "more trusting of the universe," as she puts it. Her therapy has set her on a spiritual path, but she doesn't know where to go with her new direction. Joan has long made a distinction between the "spiritual" and the "religious" dimensions of her life; she believes that the church has to do with the religious dimension, but has never had any reason for associating it with the spiritual. Her therapist is open to talking with her about her spiritual issues, but Joan finds that the therapist's spiritual life revolves around her membership in a discussion group on psychic phenomena, and that that is what "spiritual" means to her. That is not what Joan is seeking.

She has been a member of the congregation for some years, but has not been active since her depression began. A friend encourages her to see the volunteer coordinator of the congregation, the person whose job it is to see that people's gifts and the tasks of ministry are well matched. Joan speaks with her about the loss of faith which coincided with the onset of her depression. Much of her therapeutic journey took the form of questioning God and of calling God to accountability for the many injustices and sufferings of the world. Joan had stopped attending church, for it seemed dry and pointless to her, having little to do with the vital and loving God which she demanded. The coordinator tells Joan that her faith is not "gone," but changing from a child's faith into a questioning, searching, more mature faith that is on a par with her psychological journey. She and Joan read together passages from the book of Job, and Joan finds in Job a spiritual forebear.

She begins attending worship services again. At first she must do a lot of sorting, choosing, and clarifying of what she sees and hears there. She does not want people to assume that they and she mean the same thing when they use common words of the faith. She feels very separate from people that she had known for years in the congregation, as if they had no common experience at all, no basis on which they could relate at any level. As she continues, she finds to her surprise that she hears and sees things that she missed before. Passages from Scripture seem to take on different meanings, and the experience of going to church begins to offer new and unexpected strength. She has new experiences through which to understand the old words and phrases; these experiences have deepened her understanding of much that she had previously taken for granted. Gradually she finds a few people who understand what she is going through.

As her healing increases, Joan begins to seek for some contribution she might make to the church, and she is asked to help in the lay pastoral care program. First she helps with some of the organizational details, with telephoning and mailing. As she works with other people involved with pastoral care in the congregation, Joan finds that there are many who have been through significant and painful experiences of loss and growth. They are ministering through their own gifts, gifts gained painfully. As Joan begins to begin to work with them, she understands the value, even the necessity, of support from a warm and solid community for anyone doing pastoral care. She is willing to use whatever gifts she finds, and to reflect on them and clarify them with her pastoral reflection group. She is growing into a fuller use of her gifts even as she grows in her ability to give thanks for all of her life, even for the difficult parts.

Sam is in his thirties and is still trying to decide what he is going to be when he grows up. He has had a number of jobs, all unrelated, and did well in each one until he tired of it. Until now, this has never been a problem; there is always something more interesting to be done. But lately he has been having long thoughts on mortality, and has felt that he has not built anything lasting out of his abilities. He has told friends, "All this work, and so little to show for it. The pay is good, but is that all there is?" Sam is looking not for a job, but for a vocation, one that will not only call out the best from within him, but which will also help him to set some limits in his life by putting aside other, less important, things.

A friend recommends that Sam participate in Cursillo, a renewal weekend sponsored by his diocese. The friend tells him little more than that it is a "short course" in the Christian faith; Sam is dubious, but is willing to try it. At Cursillo he finds that he is not looking so much for his gifts as for a sense of direction in his life. Many of his deepest values are affirmed as central values of the faith. This discovery elates him, and when Sam returns home he begins to look for areas where he can act on what he believes most deeply. For a while he is active in the Cursillo movement, and makes significant contributions there.

Over the next few years Sam becomes more active in the volunteer work of his congregation. He finds that his job becomes less and less fulfilling, while the work he does through his congregation gives him energy and purpose. He knows that he is easily bored, that he needs a variety of challenges and activities. He finds that he has a gift of articulating his understanding of the Christian faith in such a way that others can make better sense of it. He will say that it is his own understanding of Christianity, not necessarily the "official" one, but others find it helpful. Finally his pastor suggests to him that he consider a vocation to the ordained ministry. After some months of struggle and discussion with close friends, Sam decides to try this new vocation and begins the process toward ordination.

Heather is an adult child of alcoholic parents. She has read a lot, participated in Adult Children Of Alcoholics, done a good bit of work in therapy. She has discovered and reflected on many of her self-defeating patterns of behavior which she learned in her childhood, consciously learning new patterns to replace them. Heather is well aware of most of the wounds that she had received from her parents, as well as the considerable love that she received. Now she asks herself, "Is this all there is?—just overcoming the negative patterns? Is there not a gift in any of this?"

Heather participates in a Gifts Discovery Weekend at her parish, but leaves it without the knowledge of any particular gifts that she is confident enough to claim for herself. They all seemed to be describing someone else. Heather is frustrated at not discovering her gifts with confidence, and feels angry and let down by her congregation, which, as she puts it, "talks a lot about love but then doesn't follow through." She has learned to deal more assertively with her anger, so she goes to the assistant for pastoral care in her congregation.

Through talking with her, Heather discovers that she is seeking from her congregation what she so long sought and failed to receive from her parents: steady, consistent love expressed in daily actions. She remembers all the mixed messages that she received from her parents, messages which often both affirmed and denied her self-worth in the course of a single hour. She remembers having to sort through all the messages she received from outside herself until she came to a consistent sense of who she was: a valuable, competent, caring, imperfect and acceptable person. She remembers also her conviction that every piece of her experience was important to her in some way, that none of it was to be discarded. Now she feels as if she is merely re-tracing her therapy—until the pastoral counselor suggests that in sorting out all these conflicting messages, Heather has also done much valuable work in coming to terms with who she really is.

If Heather has a single overriding personal issue, it was the question of her integrity, of psychological wholeness. She realizes that the work which she had done in therapy was largely motivated by this drive toward wholeness that she had experienced for most of her life, and that her successes in therapy had been largely around this one issue. She had also noticed that people sought her out to talk over their lives with her, although they (and she) did not always understand why they did this. She knew it was not because of special wisdom or specific skills, still less because of training. They simply said that they trusted her in a way that had nothing to do with whether she was right or wrong. They needed a trustworthy listener. The pastor helps Heather to see that here in the painful and yet fertile ground of her particular wounds, something had been planted which is now yielding its healing fruit in the lives of other people.

Discerning Prayer

This remarkable congregation that we have been imagining has found a dynamic relation between its being and its doing. The relationship is not understood as a "balance," as if being and doing were somehow commensurate but opposed and needed to keep each other in check, but as two vital parts of its life each of which is necessary for the other to flourish. The congregation's doing is centered on its understanding of gifts; its being is centered in its prayer. I'll write in a later chapter about corporate worship, especially about the Holy Eucharist and how it embodies intentional action; now I want to write about the equally important private aspect of prayer and its relation to gifts.

Like most activities, praying may have many functions. It may, for example, be a way to belong to a community, as in corporate prayer, or to express our dependency and trust in God. It may affirm our own intention of acting on behalf of God's kingdom, or to express our deepest desires to God. One important function of praying—especially important in learning our gifts—is the discernment of God's will for us and for our community of faith.

In trying to learn God's will for us, we may pray over passages from Holy Scripture. We may take a passage which seems to hold something of particular importance for us, and through meditation on it try to understand what God is about in the world and in our lives. We may try to understand God's action in the historical situation described in the passage in order to understand how God might be acting in our own. Or we may try to see how God's action in this passage fits with other passages, looking for patterns of ordering and caring. We may try to summarize a number of passages in theological terms, abstracting a common understanding from them. We may look at heroes and heroines of the faith, trying to understand how they knew what God's call to them was, how they came by the courage and wisdom to follow it, and what in their character and culture helped and hindered them in their response. In this way we may see the similarities and differences in the biblical situation and our own and so come to understand God's will for us. We may, for example, realize that God's action on behalf of the poor and oppressed is characteristically expressive of God's desire for *shalom*, and begin to look for ways to participate in that same work today. Then our prayer for gifts would be to receive and use those gifts which are useful in the work on behalf of the justice that leads to *shalom*.[1]

Harrison prayed in this way, and discovered in Scripture a call to *shalom*. He began to look for opportunities to work on behalf of justice. His own parish did not offer such opportunities but he kept praying and looking. He learned of a group meeting at the nearby university; the meeting was concerned about the people of Nicaragua and about American involvement there. Many of the Christians in Nicaragua were of his own denomination, he learned, and Harrison was distressed to find that his tax money was going to buy weapons to kill them.

Up to this point Harrison had not thought of himself as having any particular gifts, but as he continued to meet with the group and learn what was happening in Nicaragua, he found himself more and more committed to doing something about it. When the group decided to lobby its congressional delegation by mail, Harrison found that he was very good at helping the group think through what they wanted to say to their delegation, and at keeping their enthusiasm up for the task. He did not have much of a gift at organizing, but there were several others in the group who did, while Harrison's enthusiasm and clear thinking turned out to be his unique and invaluable contribution to the group. At the same time that he was discovering and growing into this ministry, Harrison kept the members of his parish informed about his work, speaking to some of the adult classes and encouraging the congregation to pray for the group with which he was working as well as for the people on whose behalf he worked.

Another way of praying in order to learn God's will for us is to pray our own deepest desires, simply asking God for what we most want. This is how many of us begin to pray, and it is honored by long and widespread use. This kind of prayer is honored by Jesus in such parables as the importunate widow (Luke 18:2-3) or the man who woke his neighbor in the middle of the night to ask for food for a guest (Luke 11:3-9). In this kind of prayer, however, we quickly run into the problem of "unanswered prayer" and the frustration and questioning (and often glib answers) it brings. Sometimes prayer seems like trying to batter down a door with our heads, and we wonder if God meant it to be this difficult.

If we stay with this prayer and try to pray smarter, if not harder, we may conclude that what we are asking for is not quite to the point, not quite in keeping with God's action throughout Scripture and in today's world. We may begin to think about our prayer and even come to question our habitual ways of praying. Our questioning may lead us into a deeper realization of God's purpose, and that knowledge then can help us to pray more wisely.

Mary prayed for her grandfather to be healed. He was in his nineties, had lived a quiet and happy life, and now was sliding toward death as quietly as he had lived. Mary loved her grandfather very much, and wanted him to be with her for many more years. As he drifted closer and closer to death, she began to question.

First she questioned God. Was God not loving? Did God not want everyone to be healed? And her grandfather was such a good man, it did not seem right to her for him to be dying, just like other people who had led much worse lives. Did not God honor good lives? Then she began to question her own prayer. Was she not praying correctly? Was she not good enough, was her faith not great enough, for God to answer her prayers? Was it selfish for her to pray for healing for her grandfather—for, after all, she was not praying for something for herself!

Her grandfather died, and in her grief she continued to question, sometimes angrily, sometimes sadly, always faithfully. She asked her friends, and they told her, "God always answers prayers. Sometimes he says, 'Not yet.'" That did not make sense to her, for 'not yet' was too late for her grandfather!

She read Scripture, at first looking for passages about healing and resurrection. They seemed so clear, so simple. Jesus prayed or laid his hands on someone and they were healed! It worked for him—why not for her? But of course she couldn't compare herself to Jesus, nor her faith to his. But he did say that his followers would do greater things than he did. Each time she seemed to resolve her questions, another came along.

Mary began noticing some details about the passages in the Bible where Jesus healed people. First, there were no "mass healings" of the kind where Jesus simply healed a group of people. He seemed to work with people one at a time. He commented on their faith, sometimes saying that their faith had healed them. He asked a man if he wanted to be healed, and after thinking about that for a while, Mary decided that it was not as stupid a question as it first appeared. Moreover Jesus possessed little power to heal in his home town, as if he had to be a stranger to someone in order to heal that person. If Jesus had wanted everyone healed, he certainly had not taken the most direct, dramatic way to do it! Presumably he could have simply decided that everyone in Galilee was to be healed, and they would have been. But he didn't do it that way. So evidently the fact of healing was not the point of these stories. Perhaps it wasn't the point in the case of her grandfather, either. Maybe his healing wasn't quite to the point of God's will for the world.

For the people whom Jesus healed, their healing certainly seemed to be of central importance. But not for Jesus. It was as though these healing stories were about two different views of reality. For those who sought Jesus' healing, all they could see was their disease and the possibility of being restored. But for Jesus, the healing seemed to be something he did in order that something else might occur.

Then Mary remembered the Zen saying: "The finger points at the moon. The dog barks at the finger, and does not see the moon." What was the moon that Jesus saw while everyone else was looking at the finger? Mary began to see that the key was the kingdom of God. As she read and questioned further, she decided that the kingdom of God lay behind virtually everything that Jesus said or did. All of his teaching, all his preaching, all the miracles of healing and of commanding nature—all these were apparently ways of dramatizing and inviting people into the kingdom of God. She decided that her initial prayer for her grandfather had been a good one for where she had been at that time, but that her new insights led her to pray differently—that the kingdom of God might indeed come on earth, and that she might be an instrument for its coming. So Mary's faithful questioning and reflection led her gradually into a deeper understanding of God's purpose, and her deeper understanding allowed her to pray more and more wisely.

She also found that her first kind of praying had not called her into response—that is, it was simply asking God to heal her grandfather, without any action on her part. In fact, she had been taught that to offer any action in the context of that kind of prayer was bargaining with God, and that it was wrong. As she began to learn a wiser prayer, she began to be more and more excited about working with God in building God's kingdom. She sensed that her own future was somehow caught up in God's future, this kingdom, and her prayer became an exciting response to that future into which she was invited. She was ready to begin learning about her gifts for sharing in the building up of God's world.

Your Congregation?

I have described a single hypothetical parish and you may have noted that it must have been a large one, with many different staff positions—youth worker, volunteer coordinator, and so on. In an average-size and smaller parish, the roles are likely to be combined in fewer staff positions and more volunteer positions, or in one or two people. But the goal of aiding people to discern, explore, and use their gifts is necessary in any congregation, no matter what its size, and the gifts for doing so can be found in any congregation.

I have told about the congregation by telling the stories of some of the people in it. The parish *is* people, people with great diversity of interests and abilities but called together in one cause. It is the cause of God in the world, reconciling, bringing forgiveness and oneness with God through the use of their diverse gifts. Where the Holy Spirit is present, so are the gifts necessary for the Spirit's work, and so are the fruits of the Spirit available for those who seek and use their gifts. James Fenhagen writes, "Every member of the body possesses the gifts necessary for ministry. The task of the congregation, therefore, is to enable these gifts to be put to use."[2]

Despite the fact that it is hypothetical, our parish does illustrate what many parishes are discovering through their attention to gifts. Everyone is gifted. There are enough gifts in our parish that we can do what we need to do to on behalf of the kingdom of God. Our gifts lie at the heart of our identity, making *who we are* available to God for God's work. They are as diverse as we are; the range of spiritual gifts is no less rich and varied than the range of human personality. In order to get on with God's work, we must have a place to discover, discuss, clarify, test and use our gifts, to become more and more converted to Christ, to "rejoice in other people's gifts and graces," [3] to find support and understanding when we fail, and to share the joy of our successes. Every parish is called to become such a place; every parish is potentially such a place.

FINDING OUR SPIRITUAL GIFTS

In this chapter we will learn several ways to identify our spiritual gifts. Our method will be like that of an artillery gunner. He makes ranging shots, his best estimates of the correct position of the target, correcting after each shot. On the third or fourth shot, he usually hits the target.

So will we. Our first shot is based on our ability to see the best qualities of ourselves in others. Our second shot will be based on our own experiences in which we have used our gifts. Our third shot is the use of a questionnaire to identify which of the biblical gifts we possess.

By the time you have completed these ranging shots, you should not only have a clear idea of what your gifts are, but you will have a considerable amount of data to support your claim to those gifts. As we go along, I will occasionally encourage you to put together what you have discovered to that point.

So. Let us begin.

I'm going to assume that you have some time to spend now working on these exercises. You will probably want to set aside about an hour to spend on these exercises after reading the entire chapter through. Whether you are by yourself or in a small group, it is best to do these exercises in a relaxed but exploring mood. Reading this book without doing the exercises for yourself is like reading a sex manual without having the opportunity to practice what you learn. Well . . . maybe this book is more fun to read.

Heroes and Heroines

Good. Now that you have some time to spend on this, I ask you to find a quiet place, get paper, pen, and a Bible, and take a few minutes to relax. A lot of this work is best done in a relaxed, almost dreamy state of mind. I suggest that you make a short passage from Scripture part of your settling down and in, and I will offer some passages as we go along. It can be a reading from Scripture that asks for God's guidance as you begin, a prayer for discernment or wisdom. Read it through once or twice slowly, saying each word to yourself, and meditate on it for several minutes. Then put your Bible aside and begin.

I'd like for you to take a few minutes to think of your heroes and your heroines. Don't write anything yet—just think. A hero or heroine is someone whom you admire and would like to resemble more. They have qualities or abilities you admire, perhaps even envy. They can be alive or dead, a public figure or someone only you and a few other people know. They can be real or drawn from fiction. More importantly, they don't have to be heroes to anyone else, only to you. Take some time to think of your heroes and heroines. Take an imaginary walk through your life and your interests and see who your heroes and heroines are.

When you have some in mind, take a piece of paper and list them down the left side of the page, as many as you can. They don't have to be in any particular order—this is a brainstorm list, and we'll order it later. Give yourself plenty of time for this; when you think you are finished, take another few minutes and see if other names come to you.

At this point your worksheet might look like this:

Winston Churchill
Carl Rogers
William Temple
my friend Annie Genet
my father
Jesus
my friend Ray Owens
Theodore Roosevelt
Pooh Bear
Merlin
Terry Holmes

When you feel that your list is fairly complete (there will always be opportunity to add more later), choose and underline the names of six heroes and heroines that are most special to you, people who stand out for you in the list you have made. I'm assuming that you have more than six names in your list. If you don't, that's no problem; just give yourself time to think of some more. If you don't think of yourself as having any heroes or heroines, perhaps a good question would be, "Who would your heroes and heroines be if you had some?"

At this point you have six persons who are heroes and heroines for you. The next step is to write, to the right of each of these underlined names, two or three *characteristics or talents* that that person has, characteristics or talents that make that person one of your heroes or heroines.

At this point, your worksheet might look like this:

Winston Churchill	skill with words; leadership wisdom; physical courage
Carl Rogers	
William Temple	theological vision for the social order skilled with words world perspective leadership based on social vision
my friend Annie Genet	
My father	humor faithfulness a courageous spirit integrity
Jesus	fearlessly confrontative in the cause of the kingdom of God faithfulness compassion
my friend Ray Owens	
Theodore Roosevelt	
Pooh Bear	
Merlin	always has a solution to the problems of others deep wisdom can see deeply into things
Terry Holmes	brilliant teacher and scholar great pastor great faithfulness to the inner journey

Yours will look different from this one, of course—I just made it up to give you a sense of the layout of the page. You have a list of approximately eighteen characteristics of your heroes and heroines: about three characteristics each for about six heroes and heroines. Now take a moment to refine this list. Spend a few minutes asking yourself what was special about *the way this person exhibited this characteristic*. If you've listed "loving", for example, ask "How was this person loving in a way that another person would not have been? What was special about the nature of this person's loving?" For example, what was special about William Temple's world vision was the fact that it was solidly based in Christ, and that he combined Christianity and social consciousness with an integrity and brilliance unequalled in his time. Or Merlin, as he is portrayed in Mary Stewart's novels about King Arthur: what a wisdom figure! He was essentially a man before his time, aware that he had the Sight and equally aware that it was not the unalloyed gift that it seemed. He was his own man, trying to balance conflicting loyalties to achieve the most good. Our heroes and heroines are special people. If they're special to us because of their capacity to love, then their capacity to love is special. What is special about it? Spend a few minutes refining the list of characteristics to reflect the unique qualities of these special people.

Perhaps you've noticed some similarities in the qualities and characteristics you've listed, and you may have guessed the next step. Look at the characteristics you've listed, and look for similarities—common words, common themes. The people themselves may not be very much alike, but there are probably a handful of themes in these characteristics that pretty well sum them up. In our example, facility with words is an obvious theme; faithfulness to a cause or a person is another. As you recognize common themes, list them across the bottom of the worksheet.

Take your time with this. It's not uncommon for people to leave and come back to it another time. This part seems to require a certain amount of brooding and staring. (We'll have another opportunity for brooding and staring in the chapter on wounds, spiritual gifts, and healing of memories.) Connections emerge slowly, and require imagination and perception to see them. Often it helps to ask someone else to look at the list with you and help you see the themes. In a workshop, people often work on this part in pairs.

When you've gotten the themes common to these heroes and heroines to your liking, take a deep breath and relax, for the main work of this first exercise is over.

Here is the meaning of what you've discovered: Your heroes and heroines bear in them the gifts which are latent in you. They use in full measure what you probably use only partially. The fact that you have identified them as heroes and heroines of yours is an indication that you and they share significant gifts.

How do you feel about that? I hope you take pleasure in finding that you have something in common with people you admire.

Some people find it difficult to believe the results of this exercise—that they have gifts similar to their heroes and heroines. If you find that difficult also, I have two suggestions. The first is simply to go ahead with the other exercises. Use the results from the exercises you do trust; perhaps the next one or the one after that will be more convincing.

Before you leave this one behind, however, I encourage you to think carefully about how much of yourself you have put into this exercise. The choice of heroes and heroines was yours, and it's probably true that no one else would have come up with this particular *combination* of persons. Then you chose the particular characteristics that made them *your* heroes and heroines. Someone else would have seen in them different characteristics than you did, because they had different reasons for choosing them as heroes and heroines.

So your personality is written across those themes that you found and listed at the bottom of the page; you have described yourself, at least in potential, as accurately as anyone could.

Put your worksheet away for the moment. In the next section we will take another "ranging shot" from a different point of view, and then we will take time to put both exercises together in a trial synthesis. Until then, I suggest that you spend some time in thanksgiving to God for sending us heroes and heroines. In looking at them, we may see our own true gifts.

Meaningful and Fulfilling Experiences

Here's another ranging shot in discovering your particular gifts. If you have been working on this in a group or as part of a workshop, the group will probably take a break between exercises. If you are doing the work on your own, you may want to do this exercise several hours later or even on another day, depending on the amount of time you have.

Take a few moments to relax. Think about the Lord's Prayer, especially "Thy Kingdom come, thy will be done on earth as it is in heaven." What would change in your life if that were to come true right this moment? What would look different, sound different, taste different? Try to picture it in positive images, not just as "no hunger" or "no war". Take a few moments to give yourself to God, offering yourself, your soul and body for God's kingdom in our world. When you're ready to offer whatever you discover in this exercise, you're ready to begin.

Take a few moments to think over your life, concentrating on times in which you did something well and had a feeling of fulfillment in doing it. They may be single events, or they may be series of events, such as raising a child. They may be from your early youth, things that happened last week, or events from any time between. They may be things for which you received a lot of approval from others, or things which no one else knew about or paid special attention to. Just let your mind range over the span of your life and remember these times when you *did something well* and *were fulfilled in doing it*.

When you've gotten some of these events in mind, list them down the left side of a clean page, just as you did in the heroes and heroines exercise. Take time to list as many as you can think of. When you're finished, wait for a few moments to see if any others come to you.

Now underline about six of these events which will serve to represent them all, six events which are your favorite examples of times when you've done something well and gotten feelings of fulfillment from them. Here's one person's beginning list of events:

Finished college, the first in my family to do so

Taught myself to cook well and plan meals

Cared for my dying grandmother

At college, organized a student catering business

The only person in my tenth grade class who didn't make fun of Rusty Martin

Sent my parents a round-trip ticket to visit me the year I was in California

Learned to do routine servicing on my car

Started my own business only three years out of college

Was part of the student strike on campus in 1970

Had the courage to break off that terrible relationship with S.P.

Learned to write funding proposals for Literacy Volunteers of America

Entered the New York Marathon in 1983 and trained for six months before the race. Finished!

When you've underlined about six events, write to the right of each of the six some of your *talents or other personal characteristics* that you used in the event. What did you use in this event that allowed you to do something well and to find fulfillment in it?

The rest of this exercise is similar to the heroes and heroines exercise. Take a few moments to elaborate your list of talents and characteristics by asking how this talent or characteristic was special. For instance, if you put "good at organizing", be more specific about that. How were you good at organizing in ways different from someone else who was good at organizing? What were you good at organizing —people, ideas, drawers and closets? In other words, what was your special gift in organizing?

When you've gotten twelve to eighteen talents or characteristics (two or three for each of the six events), and when they describe you pretty well in your uniqueness, begin to look for groups that go together. I call them themes or constellations. List the themes at the bottom of the page. It may help to do this with another person, or to come back to it two or three times.

Here's how the previous list developed:

Event	Talent or characteristic
• Finished college; worked hard to earn money for it; the first of my family to complete college	• Hard worker, persistent, not afraid to try new things
• Taught myself to cook well; especially good at planning interesting meals for a family week by week	• Self-motivated, persistent, creative, skilled at organizing, planning, and executing
• Cared for dying grandmother; not only for her bodily needs, but came up with ways to take her mind off her cares by reading to her, drawing her out and listening to her	• Patience, people-caring, responsible, good at following a schedule, listening skills, sensitive to others' needs

Themes:

- Persistence (patience, stick-to-it-iveness, responsibility)
- Sensitivity and caring for others, both their physical and emotional needs
- Creative
- Self-starter, can work well alone
- Planner and schedule-follower

These themes represent gifts which you have actually used in your life. They are *realized* gifts, in contrast to the *potential* gifts of the heroines and heroes exercise. This exercise gives a solid base of data for claiming the gifts which you have discovered, for they are gifts that you've used so often that they turn up as themes in your life.

How do you feel about what you've learned? I hope that you feel good about it.

Many people find, in this exercise, that they knew pretty much what their gifts were, and that this exercise did not give them any new information. But they say that it helps to have it laid out in an organized way, and to have specific examples of times they've used their gifts.

A Trial Synthesis

It's time to begin putting together what you've learned about your gifts. You have three sets of information about them: what you believed and knew about them before you began these exercises, the results of the "Heroes and Heroines" exercise, and the results of the "Meaningful and Fulfilling Experiences" exercise.

I'd suggest that you summarize these three sets of information on paper in this way. First, divide the paper into six parts with horizontal lines. Then divide it down the center with one vertical line. Label the six horizontal parts this way:

1. My Gifts I Knew About Before I Began These Exercises

2. My Potential Gifts (from "Heroes and Heroines" exercise)

3. My Experienced Gifts (from "Meaningful and Fulfilling Experiences" exercise)

4. My Gifts discovered in the questionnaire and other exercises

5. My Gifts from the "Wounded Healer" exercise (we'll come back to this later)

6. Some places I am called to use my gifts

The vertical lines divide the paper into "Gifts I'm Sure Of" and "Gifts For Further Exploration". Here's how the paper will look:

Gifts I'm Sure Of	Gifts for Further Exploration
1. Gifts I Knew About Before	
2. My Potential Gifts (from "Heroes and Heroines")	
3. My Experienced Gifts (from "Meaningful and Fulfilling Experiences")	
4. My other Gifts—from the questionnaire and other exercises	
5. My Gifts from the "Wounded Healer Exercise"	
6. Some places I'm called to use my gifts	

Just use this page to jot key-words for your gifts and for areas for their use. We haven't yet done the "Wounded Healer Exercise," so leave this part blank for new. We also haven't worked on the areas for use yet, but you probably have some ideas of where you are called to use your gifts for the kingdom of God. If you're pretty sure of them, write them on the left side of the page under "Some Places I'm Called to Use My Gifts", otherwise, on the right side.

A Questionnaire

Another ranging shot is to use one of the several questionnaires available which reveal one's spiritual gifts. They are usually based on the combined New Testament lists of spiritual gifts.[1] I have not included a questionnaire in this book, because the restriction to the biblical gifts does not fit the philosophy described herein. I have noticed, however, that many participants in spiritual gifts workshops trust the results of the questionnaire more than they trust the results of the exercises described above. Perhaps the questionnaires seem more objective.

The best of the questionnaires that I have found is the one by the Rev. Dr. Robert Noble.[2] He has done the required word-study of the Greek words for the various spiritual gifts, and has written questions to help identify those gifts as we have used them. In doing this, he has admirably avoided the fundamentalist assumptions evident in other gifts questionnaires.

His questionnaire contains 125 statements such as "I am able to go without children or a binding relationship with another person so that I may be more available to God and to my friends and acquaintances," (indicating the gift of celibacy) and the user is asked to check whether this is true in his or her life much, some, little, or not at all. There is a scoring sheet at the end, and each of the twenty-five gifts is assigned a number indicating the extent to which the user has used that gifts. The questionnaire is self-scoring, and is simple to administer and to score. This makes it especially useful in workshops.

With Dr. Noble's permission I have included a sample of his questions, one for each of 25 biblical gifts.

From Spiritual Gifts Self-Discovery
by the Rev. Dr. Robert Noble

By each question place a number representing how true the statement is in your life. If it is true a great deal, write 3; if it is somewhat true, write 2; if it is a little bit true, write 1; if it is true not at all, write 0.

_____ 1. I easily delegate important responsibilities to others.

_____ 2. I am comfortable and effective in projects that necessitate my being around many different congregations.

_____ 3. I am glad to have more time to serve the Lord because I am single.

_____ 4. I can accurately recognize what spiritual gift another Christian has or does not have.

_____ 5. I continue to seek out friends and acquaintances who do not go to church, in order to bring them to my parish.

_____ 6. I am verbally encouraging to those who are wavering, troubled or discouraged.

_____ 7. I am generally more excited about the future than about the past.

_____ 8. I feel deeply moved when confronted with urgent financial needs in God's work.

_____ 9. When I pray, healing often occurs.

___ 10. I do not mind at the last minute being asked to substitute for a missing member.

___ 11. I graciously provide food and lodging to those in need.

___ 12. I take prayer requests more seriously than other Christians seem to.

___ 13. I pray that I may be able to interpret if someone begins to speak in tongues.

___ 14. I study and read a great deal to learn God's will.

___ 15. Others follow me because I am offering my gifts to the building up of God's church.

___ 16. I have lost friends because of stands I felt I had to take because of my Christian faith.

___ 17. I visit people who are in hospitals, jails, or nursing homes and I feel blessed by it.

___ 18. I have been used as an instrument of God's power to bring about change in lives and events.

___ 19. I value heritage and values different from my own.

___ 20. I go out of my way to be available to someone needing support, particularly Christians who are beginning to lose faith.

___ 21. I can communicate timely and urgent messages which I feel come directly from God.

___ 22. I am willing to take orders rather than give them.

___ 23. I can help others to understand the basic principles of the Christian faith.

___ 24. I have spoken in tongues which were interpreted by another in public.

___ 25. I minister to others by helping them clarify alternatives and by bringing to awarenesss the movement of the Spirit within them.

When you have finished the sample questionnaire, compare your answers with the descriptions of gifts given below. These are summaries of Dr. Noble's descriptions and are in the same order as the questions. Look especially at those with the highest and lowest scores. Do you see clusters of similar gifts which you have used more?

1. ADMINISTRATION: the ability to make plans and decisions and to give directions on behalf of the Body that result in the attainment of goals.

2. APOSTLESHIP: the ability to take some form of spiritual authority over the Church at large and specifically over a number of different congregations.

3. CELIBACY: the ability to remain joyfully unmarried or without a binding relationship with another person (indifferent toward marriage or sexual fulfillment) resulting in more time and energy for serving God.

4. DISCERNMENT OF SPIRITS: the ability to perceive and evaluate whether what is said or done is by God or by other spirit.

5. EVANGELISM: the ability to proclaim the Good News of Jesus Christ so that the hearers are attracted to him and become disciples.

6. EXHORTATION: the ability to empathize with those in spiritual, physical, or emotional need and to be able to comfort, admonish, or encourage them.

7. FAITH: the ability to hold and witness to God's will, believing that the divine purpose will be carried out in seemingly impossible circumstances, and despite our immediate feelings, to discern God's will for the future and move out regardless of the circumstances.

8. GIVING: the gift of sharing an extraordinary propor-
    tion of one's material and financial resources with
    great joy and eagerness to benefit others and to
    spread the kingdom.

9. HEALING: the gift of God's healing power to benefit
    others and to spread God's kingdom.

10. HELPING: the ability to sense someone's need and
    to offer the kind of support which relieves their
    burden or encourages their ministry or both.

11. HOSPITALITY: the ability to welcome strangers and
    to make people feel at home.

12. INTERCESSION: the extraordinary ability to pray for
    others successfully and continuously.

13. INTERPRETATION OF TONGUES: the ability to
    make known in the language of common speech the
    message of one who speaks in tongues.

14. KNOWLEDGE: the ability to study and analyze large
    amounts of information and then to be able to
    communicate the fruits of study so that they
    strengthen and edify the church.

15. LEADERSHIP: the ability to lead others effectively in
    various areas of Christian ministry while offering
    personal concern and care for their growth.

16. MARTYRDOM: the ability to disregard personal
    reputation and physical well-being and to accept
    persecution or even death for faith in Jesus Christ.

17. MERCY: the ability to have compassion for the
    under-privileged and the suffering, and to discover
    ways of meeting their needs with an attitude of joy.

18. MIRACLES: the ability to perform extra-human acts which call attention to and authenticate the message of salvation to the listener or to help the needy.

19. MISSIONARY (Cultural Adaptability): the ability to adapt easily and joyfully to cultures and lifestyles other than one's own for the sake of the Gospel.

20. PASTORING: the ability to shepherd, counsel, and encourage Christians in their journey in faith and to take some responsibility for their general well-being within the body of Christ.

21. PROPHECY: the ability to receive clear and specific revelations from God for his people, and the ability to communicate the message directly in a given situation.

22. SERVING: the ability to perform tasks which benefit others, meet practical needs, and bring joy to the one serving.

23. TEACHING: the ability to communicate God's Word to others in such a way that it brings understanding and application.

24. TONGUES: the ability to speak in an unknown language for public edification (when accompanied by interpretation) and for private devotion.

25. WISDOM: the gifts of insight into the ways of God, into the understanding of life situations, and into the linking of the two, so that one knows what to do and how to do it.

There are several benefits to using a questionnaire. First, people are used to filling out questionnaires of this type, and they attribute some authority and objectivity to them. The information drawn from the questionnaire may be more important to some than the "softer" data gotten from the exercises presented here. The questionnaire may serve well as a check and confirmation of the gifts found through other means.

The questionnaire also serves the purpose of linking spiritual gifts discovery to Scripture. This may spark the imagination of the participants along the line, "If I had been alive at the time of Paul and had been a Christian, what role might I have played in the early church with my specific collection of gifts?"

A Time for Summary

By now you have a good bit of information about your own gifts. You have had a chance to think about how your own strengths are reflected in the people you choose to admire. Recollection of experiences in your past has shown you how these same strengths and gifts have revealed themselves in your own life and can serve as an indication of good directions for you to take in the future.

I suggest that you take some time to bring your summary sheet from earlier in this chapter up to date. If you have more information from the questionnaire, now is a good time to enter the information you have gained.

Then take a few minutes to write a summary of what you believe about your gifts. Use the information from the summary sheet, but now write in sentences in your own words. It could be that you believe and accept what these exercises reveal, and that's what you'd write. It could be that you have some reservations about part of the results of the exercises, and that you disagree with parts or need more time to think about it. Perhaps you have questions about the methods or the results of the exercises, or don't understand how part of the material fits with another part. Write it down! —a half-page about your present understanding of your gifts. It might go like this:

MY GIFTS AS I UNDERSTAND THEM NOW

I believe that my gifts are working with small groups of adults in teaching and learning situations.

The gifts which I have realized and used in the past are listening, clarifying, enabling good discussions.

The gift which I believe I have in potential is writing. This came from my list of writers in my heroes and heroines list, and I'm not sure about it. I'd like to claim the same gifts as Faulkner and Dostoevsky, but is that too arrogant? I think I'll do like Mary, and just "ponder this in my heart" for a while.

Questions which I have: where can I use the teaching gifts, and how do I test the writing gift to see if it is real?

This is a time to clarify your own ideas about gifts. We act on what we believe and accept as true about ourselves, and so it's important to distinguish between what someone else says are our gifts and what we believe and accept them to be. We'll do this at several points in our work, and we'll use the results of our summary and clarification later when we look at our wounded healer.

When you're finished, let some time pass before you begin the next exercise. So much of this work is done unconsciously, and the unconscious needs time to work on this material we've presented to it. New insights into this work may come as we drive home from work or as we hover in that time between sleeping and waking. A day or two will give time for this, and will let you begin the next exercise fresh.

WOUNDS, HEALING, AND SPIRITUAL GIFTS

We have been looking at ways to discern our spiritual gifts. Using these exercises and your natural intelligence and curiosity, you have been able to go a long way toward learning what your spiritual gifts are. In this chapter, we will take a different path. What you will learn will not help you to discover any new gifts, but it will encourage you to check and confirm those you have discovered already. It may do even more than that, however; it may help you to understand something of the meaning of the pain you have experienced at times during your life.

All of us are wounded beings. We have experienced at least the normal suffering of life. We have known the pains of life's predictable crises such as birth, the outrageous discovery that there are other selves in the world, and the equally outrageous discovery that there is no one devoted full-time to our well-being. We must endure the crisis of separating from our parents and of finding our way in the world as adults, the pain of separating from our children, the pain of aging, of losing our friends and family members to death, and of facing our own death. In addition to these blows which are common to everyone, life deals each of us our own unique set of trials, and the sum of these experiences of pain in our life leaves scars that we carry forever. Some of the wounds which we have experienced are fully healed, some are partly healed, and some may still be quite open and raw.

The way people choose to understand and deal with their wounds usually depends on their religious faith. Sometimes they think their faith means them to deny or repress the pain; they try to ignore it, seek distractions, persuade themselves it is not really important. Yet often their faith does much better, helping them to find meaning and purpose in their inevitable suffering, deepening faith through the patience and trust necessary to survive the suffering.

I believe that many—perhaps all—of our gifts may be understood in terms of our suffering. The relation is simple: if we did not have the specific set of wounds we have, we would not have the specific set of gifts we have. Our uniqueness as individual humans, while the product of many influences, is intimately related to our wounds. We are shaped and molded by them, made sensitive and toughened by them and by our responses to them through the years. Our particular collection of wounds is a kind of signature or thumbprint for us, for it is unique.

This relationship between gifts and suffering comes as a surprise to many people, who are quick to draw their own conclusions about the origins of gifts. Just as I can think of no way to prove the connection, so can I think of no way to disprove it. For now I urge you to take it as provisional, as a "rule-of-thumb," and experiment with it, using the exercises suggested below, to discover the truth of it. By assuming its truth provisionally, we may often discover connections between wounds and gifts that would otherwise be lost to us.

Later I will give more detailed examples of what I believe this connection to be. For now, think of all the people who have been wounded by the disease of alcoholism yet because of that possess the gift of ministering to other alcoholics through treatment programs. Or think of all those who have grown up in a troubled family, whose particular sensitivities go on to make them excellent family therapists. Many of the best marriage therapists I know are divorced; the wound of their divorce has contributed significantly to their skills at dealing with troubled couples. In each case the connection is the same: without the wound they would not have had the gift as gift.

Granted, there is more to being a healer than simply being wounded. One must have undergone the healing process in such a way as to be helpful to another wounded person, through insights, sensitivities, and perceptions gained through that experience, but my claim stands: if we did not have the particular set of wounds we have, we would not have the particular set of gifts we have. The gifts are related to the wounds.

To the extent that our gifts and our wounds are related, there is meaning to be found in our suffering and in the particular injuries we have borne. We can see some value in them, some redemptive quality. The wounds we have suffered are in some sense the prerequisite for the gifts which we now enjoy. This insight may not take away the pain and the suffering of the wounds, but it may help us to understand painful past experiences in a different light and may even allow us to give thanks for what God has brought out of the pain, if not for the pain itself. New understanding can bring some healing of painful experiences.

This is not to say that God sent the wounds so that we could have the gifts, nor to say that all suffering is always redeemed. We do not have to believe that God sends pain and suffering in order to understand that God can take experiences of suffering and redeem them by using them to give us gifts for the work of God. It is as if the experience of suffering prepares the soil for the planting and growing of the gifts.

Our wounds and gifts are significant not only to us as individuals, but in the larger context of the salvation of the world. We live in a culture which holds up many different ideas of healing and wholeness, and we need to seek a full understanding of healing in the context of the Christian story of salvation. Let us look at that story, and see how our use of our gifts places us in that historic context.

For the Healing of the Nations

There is a remarkable idea in the first twelve chapters of the book of Genesis. In those chapters we find first the stories of the creation of the world and then of the origin and spread of sin in the world. First there was the sin of Adam and Eve, and their expulsion from the garden (Genesis 2:4–3:24). Then we read about the sin of Cain against Abel, brother against brother, and the mark against him (Genesis 3:1-16). The stories in these chapters show the spread of sin from individuals into larger social structures, culminating in the story of the Tower of Babel (Genesis 11:1-9). This tale of human pride and vainglory resulted in God's confusing the tongues of the nations.

Then come the genealogies (Genesis 10,11). They reveal to us the fact that as sin spread through the world and its structures, the length of people's lives became shorter, until their life-span became the length that we accept today as normal. It is as if the authors of Genesis see that the spread of sin and the shortening of human life are directly linked, as if one is the cause of the other, or as if one is God's response to the other.[1]

This linking of sin and early death may startle us, but it seems to be an accurate theological interpretation of much that is happening in our culture. There is, for example, a link between the pollution of our atmosphere, clearly a sin against God's creation, and many forms of cancer. Smokers' denial of the dangers of smoking in the face of much contrary evidence seems to be evidence of the sinfulness of an addiction to tobacco. The link between sin and illness is not as direct as many ancient peoples believed—"Who has sinned, this man or his parents?" the disciples ask Jesus in John 9—but it does involve our suffering for the sins of others as well as for our collective sins. We are sinned against as well as sinning, and we pay the price in poor mental and physical health.

Yet the biblical story of the spread of sin and its results is only the beginning of the story. The scriptural narrative is the story of God acting to reverse the effects of that spread of sin and offering us the opportunity to choose ways of life rather than death. Rather than retell the whole story, I want to look at certain pairs of events from the biblical history in order to see clearly this dramatic reversal, this movement from sin to healing, from death to life. These pairs of events point to God's action in history, reversing the effects of sin and inviting us into a new way of living. It would be possible to find many more pairs, to draw a point-by-point parallel between those events described in Genesis and events later in the Old Testament and in the New Testament that point to their reversal. Yet here I shall only look at several pairs of events which have to do with the relation between healing and sin.

First, the events that tell of our origin and our goal. We—Adam and Eve—were sent out into the world from a garden, a situation of primal innocence and unconsciousness. We had been made and placed there by God to tend the garden. In the garden we were alone. There we had a purpose, a task, and no natural enemies. We lived a stress-free existence, the stuff of infancy and of vacation dreams. That is our origin, and from there we were sent forth into the real world of labor and pain. The angel with the flaming sword (Genesis 3:24), one of the more important biblical figures for spiritual guidance and pastoral care, forever stands in the way of our returning to that primal innocent state. Our destination lies elsewhere.

We are headed for a city, according to the Revelation of John (Revelation 21:2ff). There we will live together with others, yet this city will be a place of healing (Revelation 22:2), not one of fear, sorrow, and illness. It will be a city without social structures; these, after all, have been given to us because of our weakness. For instance, there will be no Temple, for God will walk everywhere in the city. I like to think that its inhabitants will need no hymnals or prayer books or services of worship! For those who have persevered in their faith, there will be no sorrow, no suffering, none of the things that plague those who walk on the earth today. Death itself will have no dominion there, nor any of its malevolent demiurges such as illness and war. In bringing about that city, God is acting to overcome the fearfulness and anxiety resulting from our primal banishment into the world of striving and suffering.

The second set of events have to do with language. Babel is an image, as Jacques Ellul has written, of humanity organized against God.[2] Men's and women's ability to communicate and therefore to organize was symbolized by their common language, and yet that language was a sign of their common origin in creation. Babel was a denial of this origin in God, and therefore of their true oneness. God's response — the "confusion of tongues," the existence of many different languages where before there was only one —is a sign that there is no basis for human unity which ignores our common relationship to one creator-God. The plurality of languages is a reminder of our true common humanity and of our brokenness and denial of that commonality. At Babel, the nations came into being.

It has often been noted that at Pentecost the effect of Babel was reversed, so that people again could understand each other's languages without an interpreter. Once again God reversed one of the ancient effects of sin. Where at Babel there was separation into different languages, different identities, Pentecost gave a new opportunity to be fully human as we were created to be, through unity in the one Spirit of God.

The images of Babel and Pentecost are especially important because they remind us of the presence of sin in all the institutions of our society—language, families, governments, philosophies, and all the other ways in which society structures itself. The events of Babel and Pentecost point out that sin is not simply individual, but also social; its reversal through the action of God is social as well as individual. God is working through the structures of our society in order to heal them, for the kingdom of God requires that both individuals and social structures be renewed.

The third and final pair of images are those of death and resurrection. The reversal of the effect of the sin of Cain against Abel, a man's life taken, was the act of God in raising Jesus from the dead, a man's life restored. As physical death was overcome and reversed, so were all its cohorts: existential fear, anxiety, despair, illness, dying.

The pairs of images could be multiplied, but the conclusion is clear: God is acting to reverse the deathly effects of sin, calling individuals and social structures to turn and live. That new life involves peace and harmony with other people, the renewal and cleansing of individuals, renewal and purification of social structures, living without the anxiety and fear that arises from awareness of the inevitability and finality of our own death.

Since one of the most drastic effects of sin is the shortening of human life through the thousands of "little deaths" we experience daily, we may expect that as God's work continues, those circumstances which tend to shorten human life will be overcome. Not only will the nations be healed, but individuals as well through the power of God's future in the present. Jesus came first as healer and teacher and proclaimer. His healing acts are a major part of his ministry. Assuming that everything that he did—all his teaching, preaching, miracles—was in order to dramatize the kingdom of God and to invite people into that kingdom, then the kingdom will certainly be characterized by healing of physical, mental, and emotional illness. Where we touch that kingdom—or in the alternate imagery of John's Gospel, where we experience eternal life—we expect to find healing. It is one of the signs of its presence.

As Christians, people who respond to the call of Christ, we are ministers of healing in the broadest sense of the word. Not only literal physical healing, but the reconciliation between nations, within families, within one's own psyche —all these are facets of the corporate ministry of the people of God. As Christians we are involved in the healing of the world's pain, beginning with each other. It has often been noted that the word "salvation" has the same root as the word "salve", and the term "healing" is often used as a metaphor for the work that God is doing through Jesus Christ and Christ through the church. This is acceptable as long as we keep in mind that healing involves political liberation and justice, the call to individual righteousness, as well as physical and emotional healing of individuals. The language of wounds and healing can be vivid and appropriate, especially to understand the work of Christ and of his followers, as we shall see. Yet the idea of "healing" must be understood in terms of God's action in history, synonymous with salvation in the biblical context, and not easily identified with a current cultural notion of "wholeness." [3]

Our own woundedness may give us the best clues to the means of the healing of the nations and of one another. Isaiah writes, "By his wounds we are healed", and the wounds are Christ's. Through God's grace, our own wounds may help to heal those of others; our sufferings may find their meaning in the possibility of the healing of others.

There are many examples of individuals whose suffering gives them the gift of aiding the healing of others. I suggested earlier that the most effective ministry to alcoholics and their families is by those who have been wounded and are partially healed from this disease. The best therapists I know are those whose childhood families forced them to learn quickly how to live in, understand, and minister to sick families; most of them were doing effective therapy informally long before their formal training began. Cancer survivors can often support others who have cancer in ways that no one else can.

In making this connection, I am not suggesting that wounds are desirable, nor that they are invariably redeemed. Wounds do not *necessarily* lead to gifts. It is important to say that people growing up in sick families may also be crippled by their experience. Noting this fact helps to clarify the role of suffering in the development of gifts. In the present fallen world the norm is not that people are healed to live forever, but that they die; not that people live in freedom, but that they are oppressed; not that their spirits grow and flourish through their suffering, but that they are stifled by their experience. Any other outcome is a graceful gift. I do not know what makes the difference between those for whom the experience is merely damaging and those for whom a similar experience leads to the development of wholeness. Although grace is open to all, it is not everyone who does or can respond to it eagerly and willingly. It is not their fault if their suffering fails to lead to something better ("Who has sinned, this man or his parents?"); rather, it is grace when such suffering is redeemed, a challenge to those who have received it to redouble their prayerful work in the cause of God.

The Wounded Healer

Remember Joan? In her suffering from depression, with its sense of loneliness, separation, and futility, she was led to a renewed sense of God's presence and a discovery of her gifts.

Sam's lack of direction was his wound; what he lacked was a sense of vocation, a sense of importance in a calling. Now he is on his way to testing a vocation to ordination.

Heather's wounds were the outcome of her growing up in an alcoholic family. There she learned to be a person with the kind of integrity that shone forth as a light for others and that allowed her to be a trustworthy listener. Because she could trust herself, others could trust her also.

Mary's loss of her beloved grandfather led her to a broadened and deepened understanding of death, healing, and salvation. Her gift of faith deepened her prayer and strengthened the faith of her friends and colleagues.

Where we find our wounds, there we will find our gifts. Where the wounds are the deepest, there our gifts are the greatest.

Most of us have known physicians, therapists, or other professional healers who were known as "gifted." I believe that gifted healers have not only excellent medical competence, but in addition possess gifts that derive from being wounded healers. In this section I'd like to clarify these ideas by describing two rather stereotypical models of healing.

The first is what I call the "technological model", where the relationship between patient and healer is asymmetric. The patient is not equal in status to the physician and there is no expectation that equality will ever be achieved. The patient pays the healer, the patient comes at the time set by the healer, the patient submits to procedures designated by the healer, procedures which the patient may not and need not understand. The patient is more passive and dependent; essentially all the activity and responsibility is vested in the healer. The healer's greater status derives from her perceived greater power: greater knowledge, greater expertise, security in an alliance with the great institutional powers, such as hospitals and medical bureaucracies.

This model is admittedly a caricature of many healing relationships in our culture, and it is not all bad. It is something that is demanded by many patients as well as by many physicians. But it tends to regard the patient as a object, to be repaired by technological means.

The other model, the "wounded healer," is quite different. In this model the wounded person comes with some competence and maturity, and with the ability in other contexts to give as well as to receive healing. The healer is herself wounded and at least partially healed, and has some skill at sharing her woundedness in a way that is therapeutic. As the wounded person shares his pain with the healer, the healer is able to feel her own woundedness anew. (In therapy this is often the occasion of some anger of the client toward the therapist, when he realizes the powerlessness of the therapist to fix his pain; could it also be the source of patients' irrational anger toward physicians?). Thus the relation between healer and client is one of moving-toward-symmetry, and the movement continues until symmetry is achieved.

When the designated healer has tapped and shared her resources deriving from her own woundedness, the inner resources of the person to be healed are catalyzed and his healing proceeds. Thus the willingness of the healer to re-explore her own woundedness results in a mobilization of the other's own resources, an active participation in his own healing.

Why is the "moving-toward-symmetry" part of healing so important? We may understand this by looking at Jesus's healing acts in the context of the understanding of healing of his day. Jesus's healing acts were normally accompanied by some social reconciliation. In the case of the healing of lepers, for example, the change was clear, for leprosy was one of the most feared of diseases and the lepers were social outcasts. The Gerasene demoniac was instructed to return to his city. The son of the widow of Nain was raised from the dead and returned to his mother. Jesus's healing was not only physical, but also social; it broke down the barriers which falsely separated persons and groups one from another. In fact, one might argue that that was Jesus's real intent. Jesus's mission, at least in the Gospel according to Mark, may be seen in a positive and in a negative sense: positively, Jesus proclaimed and inaugurated the kingdom of God; negatively, he confronted and overcame the evil forces of Satan, which are always alienating forces. The kingdom of God, dramatically illustrated in Jesus's healing acts, will be a time when there will be no barriers between persons; the world will be "barrier-free" for all. And so it is not surprising that healing will involve the relationship of healer and other person moving toward symmetry; where better to begin overcoming barriers than in the relationship between a healer and another person?

We can find similar ideas in the book *Miracles, Medicine, and Healing* by the surgeon Dr. Bernie Siegel. Dr. Siegel describes the exceptional cancer patients who become their own best authority on the illness, who do not accept the physician's advice without question, who let their own awareness of their body's needs be their best guide in treatment. They freely express their feelings about the disease, their course of treatment, and the persons who are helping them, even when the feelings are anger and hostility. These exceptional patients are usually perceived by their physicians to be "difficult" patients, and they have a higher recovery rate than the other two groups. Notice that the relationship with the physician is more equable than in the medical model described earlier, and Dr. Siegel is clearly on the side of physicians who will allow for this. Another source of healing can be the cancer self-help group, where the members can help one another with feelings of fear, anger, and loneliness.

I believe that the wounded healer model is important for our understanding of healing in the Christian context. When God wanted to heal the world, and when the prescription on Mt. Sinai had not been followed, God sent Jesus to undergo the same trials and temptations, and eventually the same death, as those he came to save. God did not send a technological solution, but a human being who was to suffer. Jesus is our image of the wounded healer; indeed the description from Isaiah which is often applied to him is "suffering servant," which captures both the paradox and the suffering of the savior's role. St. Irenaeus described well the movement toward symmetry between healer and wounded person when he said that God became human so that humanity might become divine. Jesus suggested it when he called his disciples "friends" and told them that they would do greater things than he.

In suggesting the wounded-healer model as an appropriate one for Christian healing and ministry, I am far from suggesting that the best of the medical model can be dispensed with. That model has much to recommend it: expertise and training, the full use of whatever technology is available, and the implicit statement that someone is in control of this illness, which does have its uses in healing. I am not suggesting that healers *only* empathize with those who are ill, or that training and expertise is not necessary. The wounded healer is a *healer*, albeit wounded. I am suggesting that the tone of a healing relationship should be derived from the model of wounded healer—if the model is to be compatible with the ways of healing that God seems to prefer in the world.

To this point, I have been speaking in this section of professional healers and the people who come to them. But the importance of the wounded healer model is for a general understanding of wounds and gifts, not only for those who are in one of the healing professions. Each of us has gifts, each has wounds; each is called, in the cause of God, to be a healer. Our willingness to use everything we have, even our pain and woundedness, for the healing of others, is the way we take up our cross and follow Jesus. We have not to deny our cross in the name of our own inadequacy, but rather to acquire the discipline and spiritual depth wisely to use the power of our wounds for healing. We are in the position of the disciples who told Jesus that there was not food enough for the crowd, expecting him to provide food for all, and who received the reply, "You feed them." They searched their purses and found that they did not have enough. They acted, probably without much hope of success, by collecting all the resources that were available. They offered all they had, painfully aware of its inadequacy. And then, with graceful irony, Jesus did feed the multitude, with plenty left over.

Your Wounds and Your Gifts

With that in mind, let us turn to the discovery of the relationship between your wounds and your healing. As in the other exercises, you will want to find a comfortable place to sit and a convenient time when you will not be disturbed. Spend some time entering into a relaxed quietness; to help with this, you might read a passage from Scripture about healing, such as Peter's summary of Jesus's ministry in Acts 10:37-38: "You must have heard about the recent happening in Judea; about Jesus of Nazareth and how he began in Galilee, after John had been preaching baptism. God had anointed him with the Holy Spirit and with power, and because God was with him, Jesus went about doing good and curing all who had fallen into the power of the devil."

The exercise is simple. Just take a sheet of paper and list down one edge the gifts you have discovered in your previous work. You may list the gifts you're certain of, the gifts you're not certain of, or both. Here is the beginning of one person's list:

GIFTS

working with task groups and personal growth groups

using language in ways that helps people clarify their feelings and their intentions and affirms them as responsible, mature persons

empathy with people who have been hurt

self-starter, independent

Then on the other edge of the page list some key words to tag the wounds you have suffered in life. The purpose is simply to tag them; there is no need to get back into the painful experience of them. Here is the beginning of the same person's list:

WOUNDS

mother's poisonous tongue

was only child: lonely

was non-athletic, always chosen last for games, often excluded

father was away from home a lot

Many people find this act of remembrance difficult. There is pain associated with our wounds, and bringing them to mind can bring back some of that pain. For this exercise it is not necessary to re-experience the pain of the wounds which you identify; merely labeling the wound with a key word is sufficient. If you find yourself stuck in this task, or if you discover that you are avoiding this task by daydreaming, talking to someone else, or taking a break, I suggest that you either spread this exercise out over several sittings or find a partner who will jot down the key words for you and keep you moving with questions.

When you have gotten your two lists on one page, then you can begin to look for connections between the two lists of this form: *If I had not had this wound, I would not have received this gift.* Here are the two lists above, put side by side:

GIFTS	WOUNDS
working with groups	mother's poisonous tongue
using language in healing ways	only child
self-starter, independent	non-athletic
empathy with people who are hurting	father away from home a lot

---

Notice that they do not have any obvious one-to-one relation to each other. Your task is to see if such a relationship exists.

Here are the writer's comments on his lists.

"My father was away a lot. He worked out of town, and only came home on weekends. He was terrific when he was home.

"My mother had what I call a poisonous tongue. She was not a bad person, just didn't think about how to say what she said. She would say that I was bad when I had done a bad thing. She believed that I should know what she wanted, even what she felt, without telling me about it. She also thought that there were certain feelings which were Christian and others which were not Christian, and a good Christian had only Christian feelings and no non-Christian feelings. When I read about double-binds, it really rang true, for she was an unintentional master of the double-bind.

"I was completely unathletic as a child. I had asthma, and would wheeze and gasp if I even ran a block.

"I was also an only child. I believed and still believe that there are benefits to being an only child, but there are some real drawbacks.

"In thinking about my wounds, I realize that the places where the average American male becomes socialized is through sports and through growing up with brothers and sisters. I missed out on both of those. By the time I was in high school, I felt pretty out of it, as if I had to play catch-up in the things everyone else had learned naturally.

"How are these related to my gifts? I can think of several connections; there may be more that I haven't seen yet.

"First, the poisonous speech of my mother forced me to learn to understand what she meant despite what she was saying. I had to become very sensitive to the nuances of language, and to develop a way of analyzing statements for their logic and for their effect on others. I had to read between the lines. I became a master of language communication very early, and thought a lot about how language can be used to bless and to curse. That's where my gift for working with language comes from, I guess—for counseling, preaching, teaching.

"Then there was the lack of socialization that comes with being an only child and with being unathletic. I felt like I was playing catch-up, so I DID play catch-up. I became a human relations trainer, and have discovered real gifts in that area. I found that I had sensitivity and some real insight into how people relate to one another, and could help them do it much more clearly and compassionately.

"As to my father being away a lot, I came across research some years after I had been ordained to the priestly ministry. It suggested that a large percentage of those who have sought ordination have had absent or weak father-figures. I wonder if I have been seeking a relationship with a powerful Father because my father was away a lot.

"Without the particular set of wounds which I have received, I could not have received the gifts I have."

Now try looking at your two lists side by side. See which gift seems to line up with which wound. Remember that the key to connecting elements from the two lists is, "Without this wound I would not have this gift." It might be helpful to have someone else look at it with you.

When you have finished, it would be a good time to go back to the written summary of your gifts from chapter four and extend it a bit on the basis of this work. Include there the connections you have made in this exercise. How do you feel about the gifts which you have connected with wounds? Are there other gifts about which you were unsure, which you have connected with wounds? Has your confidence in these changed?

I have covered a lot of ground in this chapter. Let me summarize.

We must understand our gifts in two contexts if we are to use them rightly. The first is the ongoing activity of God in the world, creating, redeeming, continuing the work begun with Abraham and renewed and deepened in Christ. Our gifts are given that we might participate in God's saving activity; their use requires our commitment and an ever-deepening spiritual life. The second context is our spiritual journey, which I will talk about in a later chapter.

Our gifts are gained at a price, a price that we have already paid in our life's wounds and suffering. If we had not suffered the particular and unique set of wounds we have, we would not have the particular and unique set of gifts we now possess. Thus meaning is bestowed on at least some of our suffering through our realization that it has led to gifts which may be used in the healing of others, and which, when so used, seal and deepen our own healing. If we offer what we have, God will bless it and use it far beyond our apparent limitations.

THE WORLD'S DEEP HUNGER

Now it is time to look at the opportunities for using your gifts. If our vocation is "where the world's deep hunger meets our deep joy," as Buechner writes, then we must look at the deep hunger of the world along with our deep joy.

But the hunger of the world, as seen through the world's eyes, can overwhelm us or numb us. We must guard against it by remembering that we do not view the world and its hunger as an objective or neutral observer, but as one with certain sensibilities and convictions, a certain history, and, most important, certain gifts. We view the world as one willing to be engaged with it, even to take on some of its pain. We are created in God's image and therefore are "free to make choices: to love, to create, to reason, and to live in harmony with creation and with God." [1] We believe that God is acting to overcome the world's hungers, and that God will honor our work in that cause. We believe that God has given us certain gifts to be used in that work of ameliorating and satisfying the hungers of the world, and that we are called to use those gifts in harmony with the gifts of many others.

One key to discovering where we are called to use our gifts is to become aware of the issues which seem to give us new energy and a new sense of purpose. For example, I am presently struggling with the U.S. role in Central America. It seems to me that I, through the government which I support, am also supporting dictatorships while trying to undermine regimes that support the rights and welfare of their people. Thinking about the suffering of the people of Nicaragua, and about my indirect and partial but nonetheless real responsibility for their suffering, energizes me. I want to do something about it. I am not certain what I can do, and I am convinced that much of what I *might* do would be ineffective,

but I am certain that there is some way for me to use my gifts
to influence American involvement in Central America. So at
this point I have the energy but little sense of an appropriate
way to use it.

In this chapter, we ask questions about that kind of energy:
"How is the world hungry in ways that I can do something
about, have some effect?" That question is a way of asking,
"What is my unique perspective, the ways that I understand
and feel about the world's hunger that no one else in the
world thinks and feels?" My energy for action is found in my
unique perspective. When I discover one, I have found the
other.

In this chapter I will present three exercises and a challenge. They are to help you begin to discover and draw on
the energy to act upon the knowledge you have about your
gifts. They are a beginning in acquiring an accurate knowledge of sources of our energy, the place where the world's
pain and hunger touches us and calls us to respond.

Here is the first exercise. As before, take a few minutes to
relax and place yourself consciously in the loving presence of
God. A good Scripture passage for meditation is the feeding
of the crowd in John 6:1-15.

Prime-Time Exercise

Suppose that you have been given one hour of prime-time
television time, along with all the resources necessary to fill
that time with a program—writers, directors, actors, sets,
historical documents, and so on. You have unlimited resources; you can, for instance, go on location anywhere in the
universe.

The only requirement is that the program must deal with
your biggest gripe or complaint. It might be something in the
paper that irritated you, or a situation at work, or something
you identified in a recent conversation with a friend. It is
likely something that you have felt some anger or irritation

about, something about which you've thought, "Someone ought to do something about that!"

What will you put on the screen? What is the topic? What will be the format—documentary, drama, comedy? Who will you choose to write the script? Who would you like to play the leading roles, to narrate? What would you want the viewing audience to DO when your program is over?

For example, Mary clearly has a love of beauty, especially the beauty of music. Her first thought of a prime-time program might be a concert. On reflection, she might combine that with a documentary about someone who formerly could not hear but who, upon receiving some new treatment, can now hear the beautiful music in the program. She might thus build a bridge between the now-hearing person and the TV viewer through their common love of music, and might intend to move the viewer to a deeper understanding and sympathy with those whose hearing is impaired.

Bill, on the other hand, is caught in the conflict of his parents over his vocation. He might at first think of a television program about parenting, in which the parents would be confronted with the need to show greater understanding of their son. But in thinking about it further, Bill might decide that is not the real problem, that it is in fact a natural way for them to act in the light of his own uncertainty. He might think about the pain of not having a clear idea about his vocation, and begin to dream about a world in which there would not only be a job for everyone, but a job which suited their personality and talents and in which they could find deep fulfillment. (Were he to do this, he would be very near to the kingdom of God!) So Bill's program might be about a community in which there was work for everyone, and in which the job descriptions were fluid enough that members of the community could try out jobs until they found the one that suited them.

Those are some examples, meant to spur your creativity and imagination. Now spend about thirty minutes reflecting on what *you* want to put on the screen, and jot down key words as your program becomes clearer to you. What you have written will help later when we put it all together.

After you have completed your notes on your program, sit for a few moments and hold the images from your program in your mind. Have you uncovered some of your energy? Do you feel any excitement when you think of the program, or of the subject of the program? If you do, you have begun to find your energy for ministry to the hunger of the world.

Here is another exercise in which to find your energy for change.

Compassion Exercise

Think of your biggest gripe or complaint. It could be the one you identified in the prime-time exercise, or it could be a different one.

Chances are that it involves undesirable behavior on someone else's part. "If only I could get them to stop. . . ." Spend some time describing the specific behavior that you'd like changed. It might be that someone you know is putting you down regularly, and you'd like them to stop. Or it might be larger in scale. Perhaps you'd like to stop your local nuclear power plant from being so secretive about its accidental radiation emissions.

The second step in the exercise is to imagine that "they" are not going to stop that undesirable behavior, and that you have accepted that fact. You are not going to change "them." You can only change yourself and invite others into the process of change.

Having accepted (in your imagination) that "they" will not change, the next step is to ask: what would compassion bid me do? To answer that, imagine that someone else is looking at these persons who are trapped in their destructive behaviors, someone who is extremely compassionate, wise, and selfless, someone who has within them the capability of loving these persons—yet who is quite finite and human, with the limitations that that implies. What would that person see in them? What would that person do?

If Joan had done this exercise at one point in her journey, she might have identified "they" as God, and her compassionate ideal person might have helped her to be compassionate toward God. If she had done this exercise later in her journey, she might have identified "they" as the parishioners in her congregation who had not made the journey she had made, and from whom she felt alienated. Her insight might have been that she could love those who had not and who would not make the same kind of journey, and her hypothetical compassionate person might help her to love them despite their lack of shared experience.

Again, these examples are to help your imagination. Often we have a lot of energy about "what's wrong with the world" —that's our biggest gripe or complaint. The first exercise helps us to turn some of that energy toward solving the problems of the world. The second exercise recognizes that much of the world will not change, that most people feel themselves to be caught in their situation, often comfortable in it, and unwilling to change. Where this is the case, we may practice compassion rather than blaming, but we are still called to act on behalf of the kingdom. The second exercise helps us to identify those who need our compassion while not turning away from God's call.

Now it is time for you to spend some time in reflection with these questions, jotting down key words. They will help recall your thoughts when the time comes for summary. Then sit for a while with your notes and reflect on the experience. Have you identified some of your energy for ministering to the world's pain and hunger?

A Challenge

By now you have learned many things about yourself. The exercises have given you a great deal of information, and have perhaps organized and presented it to you in ways that you had not thought of before. While your conscious self was working on the exercises, your unconscious self was also active. In fact, it was working on these ideas of your spiritual gifts while you were between bouts of conscious work, and it did not stop while you were asleep or playing. Your unconscious also has some wisdom for you about your gifts.

It is time to put together all that you know about your gifts, conscious and unconscious, and to express it in objective, concrete terms. In this section we will look at some ways to do that. The particular exercises are not as important in this chapter as in previous chapters; they are suggestions, and you may have ways to go about this task that suit you better. The purpose of putting it all together is so that your knowledge of your gifts will be fully available for your use. It is easier to act on some knowledge when the knowledge is presented clearly, vigorously, and coherently than when it is scattered and diffuse.

The reason for expressing what we have found out in objective ways—through writing, speech, dance, art—is that that is the way we listen to our unconscious self. The unconscious speaks through what we express, whether the medium is words or musical notes or canvas and colors. It speaks to whomever will listen. Usually it is other people who hear what our unconscious says, and they often know things about us that we don't know. Now it is time for us to listen to our own unconscious self, to discover about ourselves what is clear to others. We may do that by paying attention to our own expressions and listening and looking for the things we're not consciously aware of. We can also find out a great deal by asking other people, provided we can take what they say with some perspective, for they also mix in their own projections and other unconscious ideas.

Our work in the rest of this chapter will be of this form: express something; reflect on what you have expressed; act symbolically on the results of your reflection; reflect on the action. I will present one way (writing a meditation) to do each of these, but that is to jog your creativity. Your unique process of deciding what to do and how and when to do it can be part of the process of discovering your unique gifts.

Express Something

You will need several sheets of paper and a pack of 3x5 cards. Here is the task: Write a meditation that reflects on your gifts, or on spiritual gifts in general. By "meditation" I mean that you are to express a particular point of view and to persuade your listeners to agree with your point of view, and perhaps to move your listeners to some specific action based on that point of view.

Let the meditation be four to five pages double-spaced. This takes eight to ten minutes to deliver, and your listeners' attention will wander if you go on longer. Besides, the limit on length will make you write more sparingly and probably more clearly.

Begin by jotting words on file cards, one idea per card— just key words to capture some of the things you'd like to say in the meditation. For example, your cards might read: Jesus' parable of the seed growing secretly, the birth of my first child, not having enough hours in the day, the movie I saw about Gandhi, and so on. Don't screen, select, or edit at this point; just put down whatever thoughts you might have on the topic. Don't worry if they don't string together to form a coherent whole; that will come later. Just let your ideas flow into your notes on the cards.

When you have captured some of the things you'd like to say, choose one that seems to be most important to you. Then write that point in one or two sentences. Be specific. Write as clearly as you can. For example, you might choose to write about Gandhi, and your sentence might read: "Without

Gandhi's painful experiences of being discriminated against in South Africa and England, he might never have developed the personal characteristics which made him so effective against the Raj in India."

Then look at the other ideas and see if they fit with the main idea. Some of them may be the same thing, said in a different way. Some may be different ideas altogether. If they are related closely to the main idea, they may be useful for re-statements, illustrations, or elaborations of the main idea. Arrange the cards in the order you want to use them. Try several arrangements until you find one you like. That's why I suggested that you use file cards; they make it easier to try out different arrangements.

When you get the order of cards that you like, jot some other things on cards: more examples, good persuasive phrases, anecdotes you remember, characters from fiction. Put these in the stack of cards in the order you want to use them.

Add two cards to your stack: an opening and a closing. The opening should do two things. First, it should make your strongest point. If you have a story that will move your listeners to tears, by all means tell it first. If it is a startling and little-known statistic, use it. In writing, as in bridge, always lead from strength.

The opening should also move your listeners from wherever they are mentally into your topic. "Wherever they are mentally" simply means that their thoughts are probably scattered or wandering, and your opening should help them to focus on your topic. Clarity is crucial! Your listeners will pay attention for one or two sentences, but if you have not drawn them in by then, they will tune out and most likely will not tune back in. Most speakers lose the attention of their audience because their listeners can't follow, not because they disagree. They can't follow because they can't hear well enough, or because they don't understand one key word, or because there is a gap between what is said and the way it is said. So your opening should be said simply and clearly, then elaborated simply and clearly in a slightly different way, so that anyone at all can understand it. Then your listeners will be with you, ready and interested to hear what else you have to say.

For example, you might make the connection between you and your topic in a way that would help your listener to do the same. How did you find out about or become interested in the topic? What experience did you have that led you to this particular topic? Here is an opening sentence about Gandhi: "I had heard of Gandhi, but it was not until I saw the film *Gandhi* that I realized that he knew something I desperately needed to know." With that opening sentence, your listener has an event to associate with you—you saw *Gandhi*—and wants to find out what Gandhi knew that you desperately needed to know.

Now you're ready to write. Simply take your cards and elaborate on what you've written there, in the order you've placed your cards. Begin with one page for each card. Use simple language, personal language. Avoid the passive voice. Avoid cliches like the plague. Avoid the word "it" if you can; it is usually a reference to something you probably need to state again for clarity's sake.

Let your feelings come out in your meditation—the natural feelings of fear, of not being accepted by other people if you use a particular gift, the feelings of excitement at a new discovery or a new beginning, the feelings of energy and determination to right a wrong or to improve the world through the use of your gifts.

Tell some stories in the meditation—stories about yourself and how you have used or failed to use your gifts, stories of others who have or haven't used theirs. Tell about some painful times in your life when someone did not use a particular gift that you are interested in, or when they denied their gifts. Tell of times when things came out right because someone had claimed and used their gift. If you can't remember such a time, make up a story illustrating your point. Tell it as you would like it to be.

Assume you're going to give the meditation before a group to which you belong. Assume they're people you know, and that they'll be sympathetic to what you're doing.

Write toward change. What needs changing? What kind of changes need to be made? How should they be made? What is the responsibility of each of your listeners in making the changes?

Work on it. Write it out. Polish it. Make sure it says what you want to say.

Then write the ending. It should repeat the main point and should move your listeners to do something—to act on an issue, to understand something in a different way, to believe something new, to behave differently toward someone. Ideally the meditation will generate some energy, and the ending focuses that energy toward a constructive release.

When you've finished your meditation, listen to it. Say it into a cassette recorder, so that you can hear your own voice speaking your words. Better still, get a group of friends to listen to you give your meditation informally, sitting comfortably in a circle.

Reflect On It

You'll find that things came into the meditation that you weren't aware of believing or knowing. It could be that the meditation took a different tack, that it ended up having to do not with gifts, but with some issue of importance in your life. That's good information, and it may well mean that you need to deal with that question first before you can concentrate on the work of gifts. It may be that you discovered stories from your life that shaped your unique perspective on your gifts. Most likely they are stories about a time when you felt a certain way, and our gifts have something to do with those feelings. That's good information, for it underscores your uniqueness, that only you have your story and therefore only you have your particular set of gifts.

In your meditation, what was it that you wanted your listeners to do? What changes did you want them to make? Experienced preachers know that they always preach first to themselves, trying to get others to make the changes that they would most like or most need to make in their own lives. Are the changes you were encouraging your listeners to make those that you want or need to make in your own life? It's always easier to see what needs to be changed in someone else; often the changes that we need to make are the ones we see in others.

What do you hear in your meditation that you didn't know was in you? When you listen to your voice on tape, what surprised you about it? During which parts of the meditation was your voice full of energy? Where was it flat? That may be an indication of where your own energy is for this work.

Remember, the purpose of doing this is not to make a product that will please others, but to learn about yourself. Whether the meditation is good or poor, whether your voice is beautiful or raspy, whether other people like or dislike your meditation: these considerations are completely beside the point.

Listen with your imagination. Imagine someone else giving the exact same meditation. What would you have thought about them, and about the points they were making? Is it the same meditation you would have given two years ago? What has changed? What do you imagine going on in the minds of your listeners as you give the meditation? (It is probably less critical than a new writer thinks. The listeners are also usually less attentive than she thinks, for people are processing the words through their own experience and perceptions as she speaks. They hear what is in their own minds, as their unconscious speaks to them through the preacher's words.)

Act Symbolically

When you have reflected on your meditation, do something about it. By that I don't necessarily mean an activity leading to a long-term goal, but rather something simple, symbolic, something that you can and will do within the next twenty-four hours.

This is a vitally important but often neglected point, since we tend to believe that understanding is an adequate response to self-knowledge. Often when someone comes to me for counseling they express the desire "to understand why I do what I do" when what they need is to *change* what they do, by acting on what they have learned in counseling and elsewhere. It is of the greatest importance that we act so as to connect the events of our inner world with the outer world by letting them have their place in the flow of events which makes up the outer world.

In his book *Inner Work* the Jungian analyst Robert A. Johnson stresses the importance of acting symbolically on what you have learned about yourself. Writing both about the self-knowledge gained through the analysis of dreams and the self-knowledge gained through active imagination, he concludes: "We could state as a general principle that whenever you do any form of inner work and bring it to an insight or resolution, you should do something to make it concrete. Either do a physical ritual or, if appropriate, do something that will integrate it into the fabric of your practical daily life." [2]

Avery Brooke, in her book *How to Meditate Without Leaving the World*, similarly writes about performing a symbolic action as a last stage in meditation. She calls these symbolic actions "tokens":

Why, if tokens are so difficult, should one bother with them? Because otherwise your meditation is apt to end by being nothing more than a peaceful interlude that provided a glimpse of an unreachable ideal. The token brings you back to earth and brings something of your message with you. . . . The insights, or messages, you receive in a meditation are usually deep and far reaching. . . . The token acts as a bridge between the insight and where you are. It offers a chance for a small and possible step in the direction of the insight, so that you don't give up before you begin.[3]

This kind of symbolic action is especially important, I believe, in a culture such as ours which tends to value only effective action. It is easy to accede to despair, for instance, in the work of feeding the poor, if all one's actions are directed toward that goal, and if the value of the actions is based on the extent to which they move toward the accomplishment of the goal. Even the solution of choosing smaller and achievable sub-goals is not enough. What is needed on occasion is symbolic action, dramatic action, eschatological action, action that vividly expresses a vision of the possibilities of human life. There are some things worth doing for that reason alone, and not merely because they are effective.

Jesus's ministry of healing was an example. Healing those who were ill was a crucial part of his ministry. Yet he did not heal everyone who was ill, nor did he set up a hospital or a healing order or other institution that would effectively lead to the healing of all, or even most, of the illness of the world. His *primary* purpose was evidently not to heal everyone, but to call those who saw and understood into a new way of thinking and believing and seeing and hearing. In this new way, which Jesus called the kingdom of God, God reigned in the world; there were no ill or crippled persons, and there was no death. His healing activity was eschatological, a pointer to the new and final stage of world history, and a call to those around him to begin now to live in that world so that it might come to pass.

So . . . act on what you now understand.

Reflect on the Action

In acting symbolically on what you have learned, you have discovered some other dimensions to what you were expressing. You have discovered some feelings toward it that you didn't know about before, or some complexities that you hadn't realized. You may have discovered that you were embarrassed to be acting on this particular issue, that it was quite outside the cultural picture of which you are a part. You may have discovered that you are afraid of the consequences of acting purposefully. You may have discovered joy or satisfaction in actually acting on your beliefs and values, or new energy and strength in carrying out your action.

This is important learning. It is part of the creative process of letting something take form, of respecting its integrity, of allowing it the space to take the shape it needs to take. Perhaps it is necessary for the word to begin as skeleton in this way so that it might become enfleshed later.

This writing and listening is one way to enter into the creative process, one of many ways. Their common source is God the creator, and their common result is energy becoming form—a project. Now it is time to begin planning, goal-setting, and acting effectively to accomplish our goals, but it is not time to begin to neglect this process. For this kind of activity always drains us of energy, and we must return to the well as often as necessary to renew the right spirit within us. "My yoke is easy, and my burden is light," says Jesus. How can he say this? It is not because the work is easy or because it requires less of us than does secular work; indeed, the cost is everything we have and are, as Dietrich Bonhoeffer taught. Yet we have access to that well of energy and hope and creativity through the Father and through the cross, so that we are replenished even as we are drained.

I will say more about the process of discerning God's will and finding the energy to follow it in the chapter on how our gifts interplay with our spiritual path. For now, it is enough to begin. Begin with a meditation, as I suggest above, or begin with another of the many ways to creativity that you know: a song, a short story, a letter to the editor, a letter to someone which gets a load off your mind and chest, a resolution to the board of your favorite non-profit agency, or an article for the "Living" section of your newspaper.

Only begin.

SPIRITUAL GIFTS AS SPIRITUAL PATH

It is interesting that the word "journey" has two meanings. It comes from the French "journée," and literally means "daily". That is the root with which the word "journal", a daily log, is associated. Yet journey also refers to movement from one place to another, such as "journeymen" apprentices who worked one day here, the next somewhere else. And so the word is an apt one to describe our spiritual life, which is quite daily and which also contains movement, day by day, into different places.

The journey is one in which trust and caring, faithfulness and loyalty and integrity, count more than abstract conceptual ability. There is always the danger, of course, that thinking too much about it will become a substitute for living it. But it is helpful, especially for those who try to help others with their journey, to have thought about and studied other journeys in order to have a useful perspective.

I want to use the term "path" for that part of the journey that can be lifted out and abstracted, and then described. Path is the journey without the journeyer, the map without the traveler. It is the structure of the journey. Path is description; journey involves experience. For path is dry and lifeless, like a treasure map without the presence of someone who is excited about the prospect of discovering treasure. But the map can be important, too. It can locate places of danger, the regions of "here there be dragons" which are at the same time a warning and a challenge. It can locate places of fruitless searching, the barren lands of previous journeys. And it can invite and inspire others to undertake a journey, knowing that no map is perfect but that a good map is better than none at all.

The discernment and use of our spiritual gifts can be an important part of our spiritual journey. These gifts may at times be peripheral to the journey and at other times be at its center. It is important to understand the relationship between our gifts and our journey, and in this chapter I would like to suggest a relation between the two.

This chapter is more about path than about journey, and reflects on how one's spiritual gifts are related to one's path. In this chapter I want to lay out the elements of a description of the spiritual path, using insights from psychology, sociology, and Christian spiritual direction to clarify the description. I want to show that those elements may be found centrally in the Holy Eucharist, and then to claim that our gifts form a bridge between two complementary modes of awareness, the receptive and the active modes. I will close this chapter with some suggestions for using spiritual gifts as the path for a journey.

Spiritual Path: Spiraling Between Receptive and Active Modes

The spiritual journey is a dialogue between humans and God, marked by growing attentiveness and responsiveness to the movings of the Holy Spirit. The spiritual path is about managing the human side of that, about taking responsibility for our side of that dialogue. Path is the structure of spirituality.

I chose the term "spiraling" in the title of this section to suggest overall motion, to suggest that the spiritual journey is not simply a cyclic movement which perpetually returns to the same place, but is one in which there is real movement. The geometrical figure that I mean is not a plane spiral, but a cylindrical helix, the form of a spring.

I believe that in our spiritual journey we spiral between two kinds of awareness.[1] At times we are active; then we plan, we think about acting, we act so as to carry out our plans, and we evaluate our actions. At other times we are in a more reflective or receptive mood; then we receive what is about us without acting on it. Both of these are part of ordinary life. When I am making my list of things to do for the day, thinking about how to do them, getting other people to help me do them, doing them, evaluating what went wrong and right, reflecting on what I would do differently and planning the next thing to do, I am in a more active frame of mind. When I am sitting by the seashore, mentally drifting in and out of awareness, when I am meditating, when I am paying attention to someone else without thinking about my next action, then I am in a more contemplative mode. When I pray, I often begin with great activity, with busyness ("this is what's going on in my life—and this is what I'm planning to do about it"), move into contemplation (listening, praising, adoring, "letting go and letting be"), and then back into activity ("this is what I need to do next").

Often we enter a reflective mood when our usual activity is interrupted—by a sudden loss, a change of plan, something that disorients us. Then we are less focused on doing than on being, less involved with future than with attending to what is happening now, less interested in evaluating than in responding in trust to the divine mystery which seeks and is found.

Our perception of time is different in the different moods. In the active mood, we think of time as the background against which we act. It is quantified, measured by our watches, and we use it to measure our actions, for example with schedules and timetables. We say that we are "on time" or that our project is behind or ahead of time. On the other hand, when we are in the receptive mood we often "lose track of the time," at least of quantitative time, for time now seems to be in us, and we outside it. We say that time stands still, or speak of a sense of eternity.

When we move from one state of being to another, certain mental capacities come into play and others lapse. For example, in our receptive mood we may remember forgotten names when "trying harder" doesn't work, we may solve problems by creative intuition, and we may deepen our sexual pleasure through "letting go"; all these are examples of contemplative values. By contrast, when being very active —planning, thinking, carrying out these plans—we have to screen out many things not essential to getting the job done. Over time, this process of selection becomes routine and habitual. In the active mode we need to pay attention to the things which will help us to do what we want to do, and we screen out the rest. If I am shopping in the supermarket, I need to concentrate on my list and the merchandise, blocking out everything else. Yet if we spend much time in purposeful activity, we get in the habit of paying attention to certain things and not to others. We can look at a familiar scene and not really "see" it, or we can be with a person we know well and find it difficult to pay attention to them.

This habit of screening out our environment robs us of spontaneity and narrows our world. We may feel that we are in a rut, that our tastes are jaded, that nothing new is happening or can happen in the world. And we may compound this feeling by looking to even more activity to help us break out of it. Ironically, too much purposefulness is what has led us to the condition in the first place. Mystical disciplines therefore use a variety of methods to break this habit of screening perceptions and insights so that new, fresh perception can occur. These may include hitherto ignored alternatives for action, and are likely to give a sense of new life and new energy. For example, I am often refreshed at the close of a time of prayer; I feel that life is possible and even exciting again, and often have specific plans which I had not had before. I have a different sense of myself and of others; for a while at least, I can see them and myself through more loving eyes.

We may see a concrete example of the movement from action to contemplation in the Hebrew injunctions about the Sabbath. The term "Sabbath" is a Hebrew word whose root means roughly "Stop what you're doing!" The rules for observing the Sabbath required ceasing to do the things one was required to do the other six days of the week in the course of business. Putting a stop to the daily routines of planning, acting, and evaluating leaves a space in one's life. In this space one can encounter God and can re-establish one's relation to God as creation to creator. In providing space for divine-human encounter, Jews are in the active mode; in entering the space, they move into the receptive mode; in returning, they are re-oriented and renewed.

This return is crucial, and different spiritual paths emphasize its importance in different ways. It is not enough to speak of a balance between active and receptive modes, as if they were separate and distinct and somehow balanced each other. Rather we must live in movement between the two, and when we get stuck in either one we are in trouble. As Joseph Campbell suggests, the purpose of the journey is "neither release nor ecstasy for oneself, but the wisdom and power to serve others." Campbell contrasts this with the Indian yogi, who, "striving for release, identifies himself with the Light and never returns. But no one with a will to the service of others and of life would permit himself such an escape." [2]

A complementary and equally helpful way of looking at this uses insights from sociology rather than from psychology. Bruce Reed describes a theory about religious behavior which he calls the oscillation process.[3] According to this theory human beings are continually fluctuating between two frames of mind or modes of experience. In one mode, they feel weak in the face of difficulties and anxieties from within and from without. In the midst of these difficulties and anxieties, they would like to disengage themselves from their normal social and working environment. In the second mode of experience, they have a sense of wholeness and power, and this makes it possible for them to engage with confidence in relations with the world and with other people.

We revert to the first in order to cope with normal threats to our sense of well-being, threats from the introduction of greater disorder and chaos into our inner or outer world. We may encounter these feelings especially when we are exhausted, facing a crisis or accident, or brought up against our frailty and the uncertainties of life are gradually increasing. In the first, strength comes from without; in the second, it comes from within. Reed calls the process of movement from one state to the other and back the oscillation process.

Religious behavior, according to this theory, takes place in the context of certain rituals that mark this constant movement back and forth between power, empathy, and weakness. These rituals take the widest variety of forms. They include sunrise and sunset rituals to mark the course of the day and baptisms and funerals to mark the course of a person's life. Prayer formalizes such a movement from strength to weakness; other rituals such as Holy Communion may complete the spiral from strength to weakness and back again. We will see later in the chapter how Holy Communion does this.

Intentionality

Spirituality is not a part of life separate from the rest, but is about how intentional we are and how we are intentional.[4] These descriptions of activity and receptivity should be helpful not only for an understanding of spirituality, but for describing what happens to us in daily life. Later I will make explicit connections between our spirituality and our intentionality through the Holy Eucharist. All the exercises in this book are ways to be more intentional about the use of our gifts; they are intended to help think and plan how to use them. At the end of this chapter, we will be able to see our gifts in their appropriate context, as a bridge between our receptivity and our action. Now I would like to describe each of these modes in more detail.

When we act, we have in mind a future desirable state of affairs to be achieved through our actions. I am calling that a project, for it is something we "project" into the future. Our project is actual, realizable; we can picture it in full detail. We may or may not be fully aware of it when we do act, but all our activity has a purpose. For example, *owning a car* was a project for my teenage son for several years. He was able to describe in vivid detail what it would be like when he had his own car, and he was able to act so as to accomplish that end.

The project is an actual, possible state of affairs. Behind that project lies something else, which I will call the vision. The vision is more cosmic, perhaps less concretely realizable, but it embodies some of our deepest longings and desires for relationship and wholeness, for order and grace. Ultimately we cannot express it in unambiguous and direct language, for it requires poetic language rich enough to carry contrasting meanings and values. In my son's vision of an automotive future were bound up expectations of social prestige and opportunities, mobility and independence, and adult status, some of which he may have been unaware. Despite the fact that he is very articulate, he was unable to find the words adequate to express his joy at the prospect; he was moved to saying "Gyah!" and to waving his hands in the air on occasion in an inadequate attempt to convey the depth and power of his longing.

In the previous chapter, the "Prime Time" exercise is an exercise in visioning.

The project is a piece of the vision, perhaps a very tiny piece, but reflecting in its concreteness something of the grander vision. It may be a step on the way to achieving the vision, or it may be a symbolic enactment of the vision; it may be negatively related to the vision, for example an act of despair and frustration at realizing the vision. But it is related.

Having gotten some vision of the world as it should be, and having "bitten off" a piece of that vision as a project, we act in order to realize it. The outcome of our actions may or may not be the project. Our theological understanding of the gap between project and outcome may range from "If I didn't succeed, it was not what God wanted" to "If I succeeded, it was because God has created me with powers of creativity and caring and has given me the will and talents to use them" —and beyond. We evaluate the outcome of our actions, mark where the outcome missed the project, and then re-project and act again, perhaps spending some time with the original vision to gain new energy for the action.

This process of acting, evaluating, projecting, acting—all in the light of the overarching vision—is what I mean by intentionality. I believe that it is a useful description of what we actually do day in and day out, and that it is particularly useful for describing the spiritual path. I hope that this brief description is simply naming what is already familiar, for I do not intend to suggest that there is anything esoteric or original in this description of intentionality.

How do we renew our vision? Where do we receive that energy and inspiration to continue with our own intentions, purposes, projects? I believe that it is in the receptive mode, in silence and awe, that we encounter the divine mystery who alone can give that energy and vision.

Look for example at the story of Job. Job was a ruler, wealthy and powerful within his country. We may imagine that he led an active daily life, ruling his prosperous lands. Job's life was shattered, his busy routine was interrupted, by the satanic intervention which took his family and livelihood from him. In his shock and grief he called on God to appear and justify God's action, and his demand for God's right-eousness was an attempt to continue life as it had always been. After all, in his everyday world people acted and were accountable for their acts. Yet something was different in this encounter with God. When God appeared to answer Job, Job knew that his actions, his demands of God, were futile. His attempts to act, to force God to appear, had merely empha-sized his own powerlessness to change his situation. Yet when God finally does appear, silence is the only valid response Job can make in the face of the divine mystery. "I have spoken once . . . I will not speak again, more than once . . . I will add nothing" (Job 40:5). God's blast at Job is the necessary interruption. Job retreats from his habitual stance and actually listens: "I knew you then only by hearsay; but now, having seen you with my own eyes, I retract all I have said, and in dust and ashes I repent" (41:5-6).

Job's encounter with the divine had two parts. The relational part took place when God re-established the right relationship between Job and God. God reminded Job that he was not God and called Job again into the relation of creation to creator. "Where were you when I laid the earth's foundations? Tell me, since you are so well-informed! Who decided the dimensions of it, do you know? Or who stretched the measuring line across it?" (38:4-5) Later God ironically offers to acknowledge Job's divinity if he can do what God does: humiliate the haughty at a glance, bring the proud low with a look, strike down the wicked (40:1-9).

In his encounter with God, Job is not only offered a new and right relation with God, but also a new vision of creation, a new way of seeing that caring and order is woven into the very fabric of creation. God describes ordering in terms of a measuring line, the laying of a cornerstone, the marking of the bounds of the sea, managing the janitors of Shadowland, and giving orders to the morning. Like any ruler, God has the run of the kingdom; God can journey all the way to the sources of the sea, to the place where the snow is kept. God has fastened the harness of the Pleiades, has tied Orion's bands. Similarly God describes creation with many vivid images of caring and sustaining, such as finding a prey for the lioness, making provision for the raven, giving the wild donkey his freedom, and protecting the offspring of the unwise ostrich. When God is finished with Job, Job has not only a renewed right relationship with God his creator, but has also been given a vision of the creation in which God's ordering and sustaining is central. This is the essence of God's response to Job, through which Job is restored and renewed.

Similarly, our own prayer and worship is a time for entering into silence and awe, a time for receptivity to new vision. It is a time for stopping, for going aside from our every-day activities to enter an alternate awareness of time. Although we do this *voluntarily*, we may on occasion feel threatened when we enter into this other mode. We also may encounter new energy, new vision, a new sense that the world is ordered and caring and is the work of one mind and heart. It is a time for re-establishing our relationship with God and for receiving a renewed understanding of the nature of the world.

I believe that our liturgy of the Holy Eucharist is a model for entering into the "not-doing" of the Sabbath and then returning. In the Eucharist are found all the elements of the Christian path, and when we participate in that liturgy we rehearse it all—praise and adoration, confession, penitence, and absolution, oblation, renewal—the whole of the path. But there is more. The Eucharist is also an opportunity to move into receptivity, into music and the word and silence and prayer, and to return changed. I believe that this is its more important significance, for the liturgy as rehearsal relates significant time to the future, while the liturgy as movement into receptivity and return means that something can happen now, in the event.

By looking at the elements of the Holy Eucharist, we may see there the structure of the spiral movement of the spiritual path. I will use the liturgy of the Episcopal Church, but I think that the important elements that I am describing are found in any of the modern rites which closely follow the ancient ones.

The Eucharist begins with the words "Blessed be God: Father, Son, and Holy Spirit. And blessed be his kingdom, now and for ever." In that ascription is combined an act of praise and a recalling of Jesus's vision and ours, the kingdom of God. The joining of praise with the vision of the kingdom of God affirms that the kingdom is a gift and is not of our own making. At the beginning of the liturgy we use several other ways—music, silence, art and architecture— to help us into a spirit of contemplation.

Then we move deeper into the liturgy as we hear Scripture read and illuminated in the sermon. At its best this both renews our vision of the kingdom of God and also assists us in breaking off a piece of the vision as a project. The vision itself is not clear and specific enough to act on. What we need is an intermediate goal which will move us toward the full realization of the vision, and which is specific and achievable. That intermediate goal is our project, in the sense described earlier. We bring those together with our own responsibility for the project in our prayers, especially in the Confession and Absolution.

The prayers always imply our own self-offering ("ourselves, our souls and bodies") as we are needed to achieve that for which we pray. The Confession, in this understanding, is about our responsibility for our own part in the realization of the kingdom and about our failure to respond adequately to the vision. It is about the gap between project and outcome, and about whatever responsibility we bear for that gap. The Absolution is then about God's continually renewed invitation to participate in the saving of the world; it says that we are not shut out of that activity because of past failures, but are again invited into it as for the first time.

Having once more renewed our vision, we are ready for the Offertory. With the breaking of bread and the words "Christ our Passover is sacrificed for us" we are reminded that as Christ is broken and offered for us and the world, so we offer ourselves to be broken and used. Here we may offer ourselves and our intention for the coming week. What are we going to do about what we have heard and said? What is our plan, our intention and will, for the coming week? How will we move the next step toward the full realization of the kingdom before we next gather in worship? Here we prepare for the movement back from receptivity into action, but it is an anticlimactic preparation, for there is a still greater openness that we can enter.

In the Offertory of the Eucharist the celebrant calls, "Lift up your hearts!" This is an important moment for this understanding of the Eucharist, and its importance has to do with the meaning of the word "heart". In our culture— especially in popular music—"heart" most often refers either to the seat of the emotions (as in "You broke my heart and stomped that sucker flat"), or to the core of the self, understood in terms of emotion ("I left my heart in San Francisco"). This is not a biblical understanding, nor is it the best understanding of the liturgical words. Biblically the heart is the seat of *knowing* and *willing,* or, as we might say, the seat of intending. When we say to ourselves, "Now that I know what I know, what am I going to do about it?" we are speaking of affairs of the heart. The related meaning of "heart" as "courage" is also appropriate here, for in lifting up our hearts, we are offering our knowing will in God's cause and receiving courage to act on the best that we know, that is, on our renewed project. That is "faith" in this under-standing: the courage to act on the best that we know.

In our intending, in our willing and action, God meets us. The slogan of the liberation theologians is relevant here: "If you want to know God, do justice." If you want to enter into deeper relation with God, do God's work. Our action is our part of the dialogue with God; as God acted through the Word, so we speak to God through our acting. As Jesus said, "You must believe me when I say that I am in the Father and the Father is in me; believe it on the evidence of this work, if for no other reason" (John 14:11). Even when our project is not completely true to the vision of the kingdom of God, God meets us in our acting; it is something God can work with, enlightening us and guiding us into more faithful projects. Even God can choose not to steer a bicycle at rest.

Our Gifts Bridge the Two Modes

Evangelism has been defined as helping someone to discover the logos in their dreamtime—to help them to discover that God is in their most private spaces, the spaces where most would never think to look, and to name and welcome the God who is there unknown. In the same way, when we discover our spiritual gifts we are discovering the logos in our worktime; we find God in our activity, or more accurately, we find that God has provided us with possibilities for action.

With roots in both modes, our spiritual gifts form a bridge between the two modes. In contemplation, we may reflect on how we have used them or not used them, while we may receive energy and renewal to use them further. In a more purposeful mood we may use them and plan ways to use them more and more.

Therefore our gifts may become the basis for our spiritual path, helping us to move between the two modes in that spiral of call and response which gives us life. As we try to become more responsible for our part of the dialogue with God, our gifts may offer valuable clues to the nature of God's call to us, to possible shapes of our response, and to the obstacles which we encounter in following God's call.

In listening for God's call, we may ask questions such as these: What are my gifts? What are the experiences through which I have discovered them? How have I met or known or understood God in those experiences? Where have I used my gifts in the past? Where is the world's great hunger, and where is my energy for feeding it, my zeal for putting things right? More specifically, what is the human need which has fallen across my path, around which I have walked in order to avoid it?

In reflecting on our response to God's call, we might ask: What has been my experience of graced action in the times when I have used my gifts? How has God spoken to me through those experiences? When have I been challenged and confronted? What have been the rewards and consolations of feeling fulfilled? What growth in the fruits of the spirit have I experienced in using these gifts? Conversely, during the times I have experienced growth in the fruits of the spirit, have the gifts played a role in that growth? Have I used my gifts for an effective outcome?

The obstacles which we encounter in our journey may be of considerable importance if they are interpreted as resistances to God's call to us. What blocks our use of our gifts? Are the resistances within us or without? The purpose of thinking about resistance is not needless self-analysis or fascination with the self, but rather the further use of our gifts and the following of God's call to us. It is easy to become more interested in the obstacles to our use of gifts, especially if those obstacles are other people, than in our giftedness and in the kingdom of God.

Among the obstacles to our use of our gifts is the problem of certification and credentials. Often people discovering their gifts feel that they must be ordained to the diaconate or to the priesthood in order to use their gifts fully, that they must leave their present job and take up "full-time" (paid) ministry, or that they must go back to school for substantial further training. Others feel that their gifts are self-authenticating, and that further training or certification is always irrelevant. This is a sticky problem, touching on the vexed issue of "Christ and culture". If we believe that Christ works within and through culture, then it is easier to recognize and accept cultural requirements such as licensing for our ministry than if we believe that Christ is over against culture.

To approach our gifts in humility is to be open to training and certification if that is necessary to their use. To have received gifts for ministry is no reason for arrogance about their use. If someone has the gifts for, say, counseling, and if their circumstances of life are such that they are led to counseling as a profession, then they must undergo the secular training and screening which would allow them to practice their profession. The secular issue of accountability is closely related to the religious one of responsibility in community. The best kind of Christian ministry is not done by lone rangers, but by persons willing to submit themselves to the discipline—and receive the support and comfort— of community. The danger in avoiding that discipline is arrogance; the danger in avoiding the support and comfort is burnout.

Humility—the *accurate* perception of ourselves and our gifts—cuts both ways. It means that we must not "think of ourselves more highly than we ought to think," and it also means not to deny our real gifts through lack of assertiveness or false modesty.

On the other hand, we can use our gifts in many situations without waiting for permission or invitation. One of the experiences that often accompanies the discovery and use of gifts is the kind of "meaningful coincidence" which allows and invites the use of the gifts. To the person who is attuned to opportunities for the use of their gifts and who is willing to use them in modest pursuits, opportunities arise in ways which often seem uncanny. Some have even remarked that they have stopped believing in coincidences since they began the journey with Christ! It is not that coincidences in their lives have ceased, but that they have a new context in which to understand them.

One man discovered that his gifts lay in working with groups in healing ways. He seemed to have a knack for knowing what the group needed to be effective in their tasks, and even for helping people in the group to clarify and understand their problems of living. Responsible to his newfound gifts, he sought and received further training in working with groups. When he had finished his training, he volunteered to work in the local mental health center. There he met someone who was interested in weekend workshops in group dynamics, and who needed a collaborator with exactly the skills and training he possessed. Out of his willingness to begin small came a great opportunity to use his gifts.

One woman offered her considerable gifts of organization and leadership through her church and through the Literacy Volunteers. Her gifts of organizing and motivating volunteers were clear to all, and through her offering of her gifts, others were able to use what gifts they had; she and others saw her gifts of leadership as gifts for enabling and liberating the gifts of others. Her journey eventually led her to form her own service business, where her gifts are used day-by-day on an even broader scale, always on behalf of God's cause.

Reprise

A few years ago a young novice from a Michigan monastery was crossing the border into Canada, dressed in ordinary clothes. The border guard asked him what he did for a living. "I dance on the knife-edge of reality," he replied to the startled guard. He almost did not get across the border!

His timing might not have been the best, but his answer was right. We dance between two ways of being, two modes, between purpose and reflection, strength and weakness, leaning now this way, now that. Occasionally we fall one way or the other, and must climb back up.

Our gifts may help us to maintain that balance. With an understanding of them, and with a stable and wise community, we may be like the young novice, dancing on the knife-edge of reality, or like the fiddler on the roof, finding and communicating life-giving grace in the midst of the death-defying balancing act.

AT A SPIRITUAL GIFTS WORKSHOP

Although the work of discovering one's gifts is usually done in individual sessions, there are great benefits to doing it with other people in a workshop or class format. The enthusiasm, excitement, and mutual interest and support which a group offers cannot be duplicated by one person working alone. Setting aside a significant block of time helps the concentration, and the workshop setting can screen many distractions which one encounters when working alone. There is often a gentle and supportive spirit in spiritual gifts workshops which renews the participants and the leader.

When I first began offering workshops on spiritual gifts, I designed a workshop which began on Friday evening and ended Saturday afternoon. This worked well; I could go into a parish and offer it and leave. The energy which the participants concentrated into that brief period made the workshop quite productive.

The evening-and-all-day format has its drawbacks. First, it leaves the participants exhausted; in fact, by lunch on Saturday, the participants are fairly spent, and the afternoon session is usually rather low in energy. Second, the participants need more time to process their learnings; they can do the exercises in the time of the workshop, but time is also required for rumination on the results of the exercises, and that must be done in the following weeks. The result is that occasionally participants feel that they have been blitzed, that they have covered too much too fast, and they don't take enough away from the workshop to justify their participation in it. Although I encourage the idea that the workshop is only a beginning, and that they will need to return to the exercises and the results many times during the coming weeks, and although I encourage follow-up meetings to reflect on what they did in the workshops and to take the next steps, I have concluded that the weekend format is not the most desirable one. When it is possible, a one-evening-a-week format seems preferable because it allows time for reflection on the work.

Therefore in this chapter I will offer two formats for spiritual gifts workshops, one based on the evening-and-all-day format, the other based on a one-night-a-week-for-six-weeks format. Both formats use the exercises and lore which I have presented in earlier chapters of this book. The outlines are in time blocks which I will call modules, and the modules are reasonably independent of one another. There is a certain logic to the order in which the modules are presented, but there is no magic to it, and they may be re-arranged extensively to suit the needs of the participants and the tastes of the presenter. Think of the modules as building blocks for designing your own workshop, and do it as you wish!

No matter which format you choose or design, here are some suggestions. Choose a place free from distractions, where people can move about easily. They should be able to turn their chairs toward the workshop presenter, move them into small groups, turn to listen to a speaker, etc., without much effort. There may be tables for those who prefer to write on a table. With the first written exercise, I hand out a colored manila file-folder to each participant. These are used to keep together the paper as it proliferates, and may also be used to write on.

I use a lot of newsprint. I put the outline of the workshop on it, with the times of meeting, and post that where participants can refer to it throughout the workshop. I list the main ideas on newsprint and post the newsprint. People learn better when they hear something and also see it written, so the newsprint reinforces the spoken teaching. Also, they are able to take in more information if they can visually come back to it over and over during the workshop; newsprint gives the opportunity for continual review.

In designing a workshop such as this, it is especially important to work on inclusion. The more the participants can feel included in the workshop, the better the workshop will be. They may be helped with this in a number of ways: by using nametags, by moving into a small group early in the workshop, by introducing themselves or by being introduced in some group at the beginning, by singing together, by participating in worship together, by being touched by the presenter. One workshop leader I know makes a point of making out the nametags herself and putting them on the participant; that allows her to make sure the name is legible and large enough, and it gives her a chance to touch the participant. Time spent on inclusion is time well spent! There are many more elaborate inclusion exercises, but a simple and adequate way is to propose going around the room and asking each participant to tell his or her name and a little about what brings them here. In a large workshop, this may be done in small groups.

WEEKEND FORMAT

FRIDAY EVENING (about 2 hours)

Inclusion: Nametags, names and introductions, worship, singing, etc.

Introduction:

1. What does God want of me?
   Consider the question, "What does God want of me?" Where do you find the answer? (Ask for responses.)

We can find some answers from the *covenants* we've made: baptism (BCP 302-305), marriage (BCP 424), god-parent (BCP 302-305), single-status (chosen as a vocation), vocational covenants, etc.

We can find some answers from *natural limitations:* God doesn't want me, at 6' 3" and 250 pounds, to be a jockey.

But these are *general answers*: they would apply to anyone who is married, baptized, etc., and they can smack of duty. The answer to the question "What does God want of *me*, specifically and uniquely *me*?", is given largely by finding and using our God-given gifts.

2. The Book of Common Prayer
   Look at the Catechism (BCP 855):
   Q: What is the ministry of the laity?
   A: The ministry of the laity is to represent Christ and his Church; to bear witness to him wherever they may be; and *according to the gifts given them*, to carry on Christ's work of reconciliation in the world; and to take their place in the life, worship, and governance of the Church.

Note two things about this. The first is that what we're talking about is quite Anglican, straight from the BCP.

The second is the *purpose* of the gifts: Christ's work of reconciliation in the world. This is God's goal and purpose; it is what we pray for when we pray, "Thy Kingdom come, they will be done on earth as in heaven." It is what all Jesus's preaching, teaching, miracles, etc. were about: to dramatize the nature of the kingdom of God, and to call people to the choice. Our vision as Christians is the kingdom of God, and our gifts are given to us to be used toward that goal.

3. Holy Scripture
   Read Romans 12:6 ff, 1 Corinthians 12:4 ff, and Ephesians 4:4-7, 11-16. (If there is time, break up into three groups, give each group copies of one of these, and ask them to read them and paraphrase what they're saying about gifts and the Body. Then come back together and compare notes. Takes about 10-15 minutes in group, 10 minutes back in whole

group.) These are the classic texts of the New Testament about gifts; there are many others in the Old and New Testaments. In each text some gifts are listed (note that the lists are not identical), and they are immediately linked with the Body of Christ.

The gifts are given for ministry in the world; the Body of Christ is not to be identified with the visible church, and the gifts are not "job descriptions" in the parish table of organization (though they might well be used there, as we'll see later). The body of Christ is composed of all those who seek the kingdom in vision and action, no matter who they are, and the gifts are the abilities that God has given each of us to engage the world on behalf of the kingdom.

People often ask, "What is the difference between "spiritual gifts" and "natural talents or abilities"? That is a false distinction; they are not two separate lists. Rather when we are sufficiently converted to the vision and action on behalf of the kingdom of God, we will begin to see everything we have been given as resource for that kingdom. The old Adam sees God's gifts as "natural"; the new creation sees all as God's gift.

Note finally that there is no final list of gifts in Scripture. Paul evidently did not regard it as important to write a definitive list. I suspect that there is some spiritual significance to that, in that the shape of the mission is new in each age, according to the needs of that age, and the gifts given are always appropriate to the mission of the age.

4. Our purpose and method in this workshop.

Our *purpose* is: (from above). (Check it out with the participants: is this what you were expecting when you came? Any changes we need to make in the statement of purpose?)

Our *method* is like ranging shots in artillery fire. We fire a shot, see where it lands, correct our aim, fire another, etc. It may take several shots to zero in. Our first shot will be fired tonight, several others in the morning. Each shot involves collecting some information from you. After each shot, we'll take some time to put together all the information we've collected to that point. When we finish, you will have not only identified your gifts, but will have a data base for your identification.

The process is open-ended. We'll begin it tonight, but it may be something you will want to continue to work on for a long time. It can well serve as the focus of one portion of your spiritual journey.

One more point: We are much like automobile batteries when it comes to finding and using our spiritual gifts. A battery on a store shelf has no power, no energy. If you add acid, it has some energy, but it will lose it unless it is used, connected into an automobile's electrical system. Discovering our gifts for ministry is like adding acid; there's some energy, power, excitement there. But some connection must be made with others and the gifts must be used if the life is to be kept up.

Frederick Buechner has written about our gifts, which indicate our vocation, in this way. (Read Buechner quote on "Vocation" *ad lib*, being sure to include the final sentence:

"VOCATION. It comes from the Latin word *vocare*, to call, and means the work a man is called to by God.

"There are all different kinds of voices calling you to all different kinds of work, and the problem is to find out which is the voice of God rather than of Society, say, or the Superego, or Self-Interest.

"By and large a good rule for finding out is this. The kind of work God usually calls you to is the kind of work (a) that you most need to do and (b) that the world most needs to have done. If you really get a kick out of your work, you've presumably met requirement (a), but if your work is writing TV deodorant commercials, the chances are you've missed requirement (b). On the other hand, if your work is being a doctor in a leper colony, you have probably met requirement (b), but if most of the time you're bored and depressed by it, the chances are you have not only bypassed (a) but probably aren't helping your patients much either.

"Neither the hair shirt or the soft birth will do. The place God calls you to is the place where your deep gladness and the world's deep hunger meet."—from *WISHFUL THINK-ING*, Frederick Buechner.

So what we'll be working on concerns not only the world's deep hunger for reconciliation, for the kingdom of God, but also taps into our deepest gladness. Our task is both to find our deep gladness and also to find the world's deep hunger.

Now to work.

5. Exercise: HEROES AND HEROINES.

(Distribute wing-folders or file folders and blank paper.)

I want you to list 10 of your personal heroes, male or female. They may be alive or dead, people you have known personally or not, real or fictional. (Wait about 10 minutes; encourage. Then ask for a representative calling-out of heroes; this helps some to list more than they had.)

Now narrow the list down to six of your most favorite ones, and list 3-5 characteristics of each one that makes him or her a favorite of yours. (About ten minutes)

Now find a partner to work with, and move so that you can talk together easily. (Time to pair and move)

I want you to share with each other your heroes and heroines and the characteristics you have listed, and help each other find patterns or similarities in your lists. The goal is to come up with a few personal qualities or talents or characteristics which summarize your whole list of heroes or heroines.

As you do this, be as specific as you can, and help each other to be specific. If you put that someone was "loving", for instance, get a lot more specific than that: what is there about this person's "lovingness" that would be unlike another person's "lovingness"? etc. Begin now. (Allow 30 minutes for this. Encourage, restate the task, answer questions.)

How'd you do? Are you coming up with the summary lists? OK, here's the tag for this exercise: *Your heroes/heroines have in full measure what lies in you as potential.* They use and use well the very gifts and talents you have lying dormant within—or have not used as well as you need to in order to live a more abundant, fulfilling life (Buechner's "deepest gladness"). You have these gifts within you—otherwise, they would not have "hooked" you into taking these persons as heroes.

They are our first look into our spiritual gifts, our first ranging shot. We'll check this tentative list of your spiritual gifts in several ways tomorrow.

(End with singing, compline, a film, etc.)

SATURDAY MORNING

1. From the individual's point of view.
   (This and the following exercise take about an hour.)
   (Read and comment on the Gordon Cosby quote:
   "We are not sent out into the world in order to make people good. We are not sent to encourage them to do their duty. The reason people have resisted the Gospel is that we have gone out to make people good, to help them do their duty, to impose new burdens on them, rather than calling forth the gift which is the essence of the person himself. . . . They can be what in their deepest hearts they know that they were intended to be, they can do what they were meant to do. As Christians, we can be heralds of these good tidings. . . . We begin by exercising our own gifts. The person who is having the time of his life doing what he is doing has a way of calling forth the deeps of another. Such a person is Good News. He is not *saying* the Good News. He *is* the Good News. He is the embodiment of the freedom of the new humanity. The person who exercises his own gift in freedom can allow the Holy Spirit to do in others what he wants to do." From *HANDBOOK FOR MISSION GROUPS*, Gordon Cosby, Word Press)

We're talking from a personal, individual point of view right now—we'll talk from a corporate point of view later. The point here is the same as Buechner's: to find and exercise your gifts is to find your deepest gladness; it is to *be* the Good News, to embody the freedom of the New Humanity. It is to find new life, new energy, a new sense of purpose and meaning. It is to participate in what Jesus talked about in so many ways: the great feast, the kingdom of God, the kingdom of Heaven, the eternal life.

Note that this is very different from what I grew up with about the duty of a Christian: it was to help people. The idea is basically a good one, but too often it devolves to doing for someone else what they can do for themselves, or doing something *to* someone else for their own good. Cosby's idea is that we follow our own gifts, touch our own deep gladness, follow our own path into God, and others WILL be "helped" in precisely the ways they most need to be helped: to find and use their own gifts, and touch their own deep gladness.

2. Exercise: FULFILLING EVENTS

(Make sure everyone has something to write on and with.)

I want you to list 10 events during your life in which you *did something well* and *found a lot of fulfillment in doing it.* (Repeat underlined parts.) (Take 10 minutes)

Now, as last evening, I want you to choose about six of these to work with, and alongside each one, list 3-5 talents or personal characteristics which you used in doing it. (15 minutes)

Now find a partner, someone you'd like to work with, preferably not your spouse. You are to do for your partner roughly what a good consultant would do: press for clarity, for concreteness, try to draw out the other person, and look for patterns, connections in the data you've listed. You should end this session with a good list of skills that you used during these events, and your partner should also have a good list. Get these on paper! (15 minutes)

Now find one or two other pairs of partners and share what you see emerging as your gifts. You now have information of two types, two ranging shots: your potential from our work last night, and the fulfilling events from this morning. (25 minutes)

Anyone want to share what they're finding with the whole group?

3. Exercise: PRIME TIME (This exercise takes about an hour.)

Now for a third ranging shot. You have been given an hour of prime television time to address over 50 million Americans on your biggest gripe or deepest concern. Everything you will need is provided: writers, production crew, etc. What will you put on the screen? What will you say, and how will you say it . . . drama, documentary, comedy, fantasy . . . ? Who do you want in the cast? As always, get it on paper. (Work alone for about 15 minutes.)

Now share it with your partner. (15 minutes)

Now share it with the group of 2-3 pairs. (25 minutes)

(Possible variation: share your *partner's* TV special with the group.)

Anyone want to share what you're finding with the whole group? (5 minutes—cut it off, if necessary.)

4. From the church's point of view.

So far we've talked about spiritual gifts mostly from the individual's point of view. Now for the church's point of view.

The gifts are not to be thought of as job descriptions for the parish organization table. They may find use in the formal organization table of the parish or outside it. Remember that our mission is in the world, and likely not in the parish. *The work of the church is not church work!*, but the kingdom of God.

I believe that two points are important here. One is that the implicit promise in the doctrine of spiritual gifts is that the body of Christ (not the visible church, remember?) will always have the resources it needs to accomplish its mission. If it needs evangelists, it will have them, etc. Incidentally, some studies have shown that about 10% of any congregation has the gift of evangelism. The other 90% use their gifts and in so doing support that 10%. Do you know what the purpose or mission statement of your congregation is? If you don't know that, how do you know what gifts are necessary for it to accomplish its mission?

The second point is this: that one of the main functions of the church (Gordon Cosby says *the* function) is to call out the gifts of its members—to identify them and to provide some arenas for their use.

Optional, if there is time: St. John's Church of Idaho Falls, Idaho, has used the gifts of its members in the parish organization table. They used to elect Vestry members in the traditional way, by defining roles and job descriptions: the Junior Warden is in charge of the buildings and grounds, etc. Then they began simply listing the gifts necessary for filling each of the slots, recruited people with those gifts, and affirmed them by acclamation!

5. Exercise: QUESTIONNAIRE (Takes about an hour.)

Here's another ranging shot. It is self-scoring, with no time limit.

Take some time to fill out and score the questionnaire. Then look at your top three scores and also at your lowest three scores. I'll give you a list of definitions of biblical gifts when you're through.

(Take whatever time is necessary. If they don't understand the results, suggest that they work backward and look at the questions they marked to get to the gifts they had.)

Now take some time to bring together the four sets of information you have gathered: from your heroes/heroines, fulfilling events, prime-time exercise, and the questionnaire. Do some refining. What are your gifts? Are you using them? Where is your energy for engaging the world on behalf of the kingdom of God (look especially at the prime-time exercise to find your energy). What are you doing about your biggest gripe or complaint? How can you use your gifts to do something about it? Again: Get it in writing!

LUNCH AND BREAK

SATURDAY AFTERNOON

1. Exercise : WOUNDED HEALER (Takes about one hour.)

We've gotten a good idea of our gifts, and have gotten a considerable amount of data to support our insights. Now I want to go deeper and to *root* and *anchor* these discoveries in the firm ground of our souls. I'm going to speak for a few minutes of our gifts in different terms, in terms of our woundedness and our healing.

We are all wounded persons, and our greatest gifts are intimately related to our wounds. The wounds might be physical, emotional, etc. They may have been healed fully or partially, or they may still be pretty open, unhealed.

We are also called to be healers for others, whether friend, a family member, or some group of people. When we say that Jesus is Savior, we are saying that he is a healer — that's one of the things "savior" means. The other is liberator, or free-er. So we are called to heal and to liberate or free others in the name of Christ.

Now there are two models for healing in our culture. They are both stereotypes, as I will describe them, and I'm going to exaggerate both to try to make the contrasts clearer.

The first model for healing I'm calling the "old medical model" just to try to honor the newer physicians who are breaking out of it. It is the model that goes like this: If you are sick or wounded, and you come to me for healing, then I have the resources to heal you, and you have no resources, only the wounds or sickness. You are passive, and I do something to you, and you get better. You have no role to play, no responsibility for your own situation or for its resolution.

Now even though that's a stereotype, and a negative one at that as I've described it, it has its merits. It works! Look, for example, at the placebo effect!

There is another model which I think is much nearer to the spirit of Christ for healing. It is the "wounded healer" model. It goes like this: if you are wounded, in need of healing, and you come to me for healing, you come with full integrity and resources. We are both wounded, both have experienced some healing. What do I do? In some way, I open my own wound; I talk about it, remember it, share with you what I have learned from it; I become more like you than unlike you. When I am able to do this, MY woundedness calls out YOUR healer within you, and your healing can take place.

Who is to heal an alcoholic but a recovering alcoholic? Why are most marriage counselors divorced? Who is to heal a depressed person but one who has been healed of depression?

Isaiah says, "By his wounds we are healed," and we take that as referring to Christ, Healer. I believe that, "By our wounds, others may be healed." Specifically, I believe that:

1) Our ability to heal —our gift — is intimately related to our healed woundedness.
2) To find our powerful gift, we must look at our very wounds.
3) By doing this, we may be able to give thanks for what we have previously regarded as a simple, unredeemed woundedness. The thanksgiving, in a sense, seals the healing.

(Give personal example of wounded healer. Emphasize that there are graces as well as wounds, but that we are emphasizing the wounds for the purpose of healing.)

Now take some paper and list down one side the gifts that you have discovered and are willing to claim as your own, and down the other side of the page as many of your wounds as you can come up with. Just list a key word to tag the wound. I encourage you to stick with this; thinking about our wounds is painful, and the temptation to stop is strong.

You don't need to re-live the wounds or to get back into them emotionally; just list them by key word.

Then, with a partner, begin looking for connections between the gifts and the wounds. Here is the sentence to connect them: If I had not had this wound, I would not have this gift. Draw lines to mark the connections as you make them. Here, as always, you don't need to share with the other person what you don't want to. (Take the remainder of the hour.)

2. Putting It All Together

Lets take some time now to put together what you know about your gifts. In writing:

1) What are they?
2) Where have you been using them?
3) Where do you intend to use them in the future?
4) What do you intend to do about the isues and values expressed in the prime time exercise, i.e. your biggest gripe or complaint?
5) What will it take (training? support? recognition?) to fully develop and use your gifts?
6) What is your distinctive perspective on the issues from "prime time"?
7) Finally, what is your next step in discovering, claiming, and using your gifts?

3. Some Final Comments.

Think about the parable of the talents. Two points: First, the servants had no choice about whether to receive the talents or how many talents to receive. Their only choice was what to do with the talents they had received.

Second: What kept the man with one talent from his stewardship of that talent? His perception of his boss, which included fear of the boss. We might call it resistances, snares of the devil, or something else. But: if our gifts tell us what God wants of us, then our fears, our resistances—*whatever* gets in the way of our using our gifts—gives us a clue to the working of sin in our lives. Our "resistances" are to be dealt with like any other sinful influences, gently and remorse-lessly. Thus our gifts and our resistances to using our gifts are right at the center of our spiritual struggles, and might be the focus of some good attention to our spiritual life.

As you deal with these gifts, be aware of visions, dreams, and meaningful coincidences. When we claim our gifts and begin to use them intentionally, interesting things begin to happen.

Finally, remember that the key to this exploration is what Buechner said: your deep gladness, the world's deep hunger. Follow that and you're on the right track.

Close with worship and evaluation.

WEEKNIGHT FORMAT

Here I will briefly list the outline for six week-night sessions of about one and one-half hours each. The modules are as above. Each week, the session would include:

> Inclusion
> Lore presentation
> Exercise
> Time for reflection and summary
> Worship

On the first evening, the inclusion would be more extensive; at subsequent meetings, some "touching base" is usually all that is necessary.

Session I

> Inclusion
> Purpose statement and assent
> Method
> Time blocks—outline of all six sessions
> "What does God want of me?"—from Friday evening
>   session, above
> Heroes and heroines exercise—from Friday evening
>   session, above
> Time for summary
> Close with worship

Session II

> Inclusion, checking-in from last time—"Any reflections on what we did last week? Did you learn anything that surprised you last week? . . . Are you ready to go on and take the next step in discovering and using your gifts?"
> Bible study, from Friday evening session above
> Fulfilling events exercise, from Saturday morning session above

Time for summary
Worship

Session III

Inclusion, as in Session II
Prayer Book lore, from Friday night session above
Questionnaire on spiritual gifts
Time for summary
Worship

Session IV

Inclusion
Wounded Healer exercise
Time for summary and reflection
Worship

Session V

Inclusion
Lore: "From the Church's point of view"—from
    Saturday session, above
Prime Time exercise
Time for summary and reflection—Where is God
    calling you to work for his cause in the world?
    Where does the world's deep hunger touch your
    deep joy?
Worship

Session VI

Inclusion
Putting it all together
Some final comments

What is YOUR next step?
  Ask people what they intend to do next; what they
  need; what they expect from the church; if they
  want to team up with someone else in the workshop in a support team or group, etc.
Celebrate with final Eucharist, offering "ourselves,
  our souls and bodies," INCLUDING AND ESPE-
  CIALLY our gifts.

NOTES

Chapter One: Asking the Right Questions

1. I am here following Tilden Edwards' fine discussion in his book, *Spiritual Friend*.

Chapter Two: Spiritual Gifts in Christian Tradition

1. E.E. Ellis, article "Spiritual Gifts", in the Supplemental Volume of *The Interpreter's Dictionary of the Bible*, p. 541.

2. I Corinthians 14:26.

3. Hans Conzelman, *History of Primitive Christianity*, Chapters III, IV, and VI.

4. *The Book of Common Prayer*, p. 855.

5. Gordon Cosby, *Handbook for Mission Groups*.

6. Frederick Buechner, *Wishful Thinking*.

Chapter Three: Spiritual Gifts Today

1. For a fine discussion of the relation of justice to shalom, see Perry B. Yoder's *SHALOM: The Bible's Word for Salvation, Justice, and Peace*.

2. James C. Fenhagen, *Mutual Ministry*, p. 100.

3. From the positive statement of the Ten Commandments in the Catechism of *The Book of Common Prayer*, p. 848.

Chapter Four: Finding Our Spiritual Gifts

1. On the New Testament spiritual gifts, see Goetchius and Price, *The Gifts of God*, and Noble's outline listed in the reference list.

2. Robert Noble, *Spiritual Gifts Self-Discovery*.

Chapter Five: Wounds, Healing, and Spiritual Gifts

1. Gerhard von Rad, *Old Testament Theology, Volume I*, p. 158.

2. Jacques Ellul, *The Meaning of the City*.

3. James Fenhagen, *Invitation to Holiness*, p. 4.

Chapter Six: The World's Deep Hunger

1. *The Book of Common Prayer* of the Episcopal Church, p. 845.

2. Robert Johnson, *Inner Work*, p. 196.

3. Avery Brooke, *How to Meditate Without Leaving the World*, p. 38.

Chapter Seven: Spiritual Gifts as Spiritual Path

1. In describing bimodal consciousness, I am following Arthur J. Deikman, "Bimodal Consciousness and the Mystical Experience", *Symposium on Consciousness* by Philip R. Lee, Robert E. Ornstein, Charles Tart, Arthur Deikman, and David Galin (Viking Penguin Inc., 1976). Reprinted in Woods, Richard, O.P., ed., *Understanding Mysticism*, (Doubleday Image Books, 1980). Many have written about bimodal consciousness; I particularly like Deikman's emphasis that both are normal modes and his defense of mysticism against charges that it is pathological.

2. Campbell, Joseph, *Myths to Live By*, p. 227 (Viking Press, 1972).

3. Reed, Bruce, *The Task of the Church and the Role of its Members* (The Grubb Institute, 1975). Reprinted by The Alban Institute, 1984.

4. In my description of intentionality I am following the article "An Outline of an Intentional Theory of Ministry" by Urban T. Holmes, St. Luke's Journal of Theology, March 1977, volume XX, Number 2.

REFERENCE LIST

Brooke, Avery, *How to Meditate Without Leaving the World*, The Seabury Press, 1979.

Buechner, Frederick, *Wishful Thinking*, Harper & Row, 1973.

Conzelmann, Hans, *History of Primitive Christianity*, tr. John E. Steely, Abingdon Press, 1973.

Cosby, Gordon, *Handbook for Mission Groups*, Word Press, 1975.

Edwards, Tilden, *Spiritual Friend*, Paulist Press, 1980.

Ellul, Jacques, *The Meaning of the City*, William B. Eerdmans Pub. Co., 1970.

Fenhagen, James, *Invitation to Holiness*, Harper & Row, 1985.

—— *Mutual Ministry*, The Seabury Press, 1977.

Ford, George A., and Gordon L. Lippitt, *PLANNING YOUR FUTURE: A Workbook for Personal Goal Setting*, University Associates, 1982.

Goetchius, Eugene V.N., and Charles P. Price, *The Gifts of God*, Morehouse Barlow, 1984.

Hahn, Celia Allison, James R. Adams, Anne Gavin Amy, *My Struggle to be a Caring Person*, The Alban Institute, Inc., 1981.

Hahn, Celia Allison, James R. Adams, Anne Gavin Amy, Barton M. Lloyd, *What Do I Have to Offer?*, The Alban Institute, Inc., 1983.

Haldane, Jean, *MINISTRY EXPLORATIONS: A Total Ministry Support System: a Manual for Leaders*, Renewal Press, 4502 54th Ave. N.E., Seattle, WA 98105.

Johnson, Robert, *Inner Work*, Harper & Row, 1986.

Koenig, John, *CHARISMATA: God's Gifts for God's People*, The Westminster Press, Philadelphia, 1978.

Noble, Robert D., *Spiritual Gifts Self-Discovery*, available from Gather-The-Family Institute, P.O. Box 26333, San Diego CA, 92126.

O'Connor, Elizabeth, trilogy on the spiritual life: *Our Many Selves*, Harper & Row, 1971; *Search for Silence*, Word Books, 1972; *Eighth Day of Creation*, Word Books, 1971.

Pierce, The Rev. Robert K., *MATERIAL FOR A WORKSHOP IN SPIRITUAL GIFTS AND TALENTS*, The Diocese of Tennessee, 808 Broadway, Nashville TN 37203. Leader's Manual: $5.00; participant's packet: $3.00.

von Rad, Gerhard, *Old Testament Theology, vol. I*, tr. D.M.G. Stalker, Harper & Row, 1962.

Westerhoff, John, *Will Our Children Have Faith?*, Seabury Press, 1983.

Yoder, Perry B., *SHALOM: The Bible's Word for Salvation, Justice, and Peace*, Faith and Life Press, Newton, Kansas, 1987.